The Beauty I Have Seen

A Trilogy

Malthouse African Poetry

The Beauty I Have Seen
A Trilogy

by

Tanure Ojaide

malthouse 𝒳𝒫

Malthouse Press Limited

Lagos, Benin, Ibadan, Jos, Port-Harcourt, Zaria

Malthouse Press Limited
43 Onitana Street, Off Stadium Hotel Road
Off Western Avenue, Surulere, Lagos
E-mail: malthouse_press@yahoo.com
malthouselagos@gmail.com
Tel: +234-(0)802 600 3203

© Tanure Ojaide 2010
First Published 2010
ISBN 978-978-8422-29-7

Distributors:
African Books Collective Ltd
Email: abc@africanbookscollective.com
Website: http://www.africanbookscollective.com

The Poems

I   The Beauty I Have Seen

When the muse gives the minstrel a nod
The minstrel smiles, swaggers
The minstrel's livery
The minstrel's honour
The market is a thronged crossroads
Without a guide
The minstrel comes to a river
The minstrel is a fisherman
The minstrel harps at the beach of Negril
I knew you were pregnant
For Mbwidiffu
The muse sends me to the market
The minstrel is a refugee
The minstrel wails
Today
The minstrel tells tales
The minstrel looks toward dawn
Self-portrait
The loan
Stardom
Highland dreams
Waiting
Think again
Alligator choices
Supreme artist
Bonfire

II   Doors of the Forest

III   Flow & Other Poems

I

The Beauty I Have Seen

For Ovie Ojaide:

in his special place.

"A dancer knows fatigue only after performance."

(from an *udje* dance song)

Should a hunter for carrying his dream in a big bag to the bush
brag about game that is now a porcupine and soon an ancestor?

When the muse gives the minstrel a nod

When the muse gives the minstrel a nod,
no bead ever competes with his diamond.

The minstrel gets his share of pain and joy
that he converts into songs of the season—

with the gift, an elixir, he cures migraines of misery;
for sure a wizard, he sees without strain in the dark.

He takes the impassable road to the pagoda within,
knowing the wide road without a sign runs into peril.

He matches divine favours with a record sacrifice,
carries what is light to lift but heavy on the head.

Transported into primeval rapture by the zeal for song,
he knocks out others for a singular vision of beauty.

There is only one moon, the world's munificent bride;
beside her, legions of attendants in their livery of light.

Since there is only one muse in the pantheon
and music comes from the breath of her love,

when the muse gives the minstrel a nod,
no bead ever competes with his diamond.

The minstrel smiles, swaggers

The minstrel smiles, swaggers, and glows
that they hear his songs in Canada and Nsukka;

the songs cross lonely crossroads of Cross River,
they shepherd the lost traveller to his destination.

The songs play on lips of the retinue of water spirits
escorting the water-maid to the depths of the Atlantic.

Army ants pick his work songs for their marching tunes,
eagles wing their way across the sky lisping his songs.

The fearful heart passes the long dark stretch of road
singing his scare songs to keep evil djinns far away.

The minstrel now believes his songs conceive,
induce labour, and deliver beautiful offspring;

he believes his songs lend hands to the disabled
to overcome challenges and fend for themselves.

He believes his song is the lion's speech that goes
uninterrupted by others of the forest population;

surely he believes he stands so erect in his fate
that he is the iroko that no other tree can dwarf.

The minstrel wraps himself with brocades of smiles,
believing that even the deaf nod noisily to his notes;

he bows to the deafening applause of a phantom crowd
of adulators now delirious with the rhythm of his songs;

he believes witches raze their own coven with his fire songs,
and robbers return their loot singing his songs of restitution.

He believes the house in which the politicians carouse
burns without smoke, and Abuja is only buying time.

But the muse nudges the braggart to break his swagger-stick
gilded with wax so combustible it can disappear in seconds;

the muse gestures to the minstrel to narrow his wide grin
that more than covers his scars, smudges, and splotches.

The bemused muse whispers a sagely message:
Come down the high roof of the house of words;

move away from the hurricane alley to a safe ground.
Come down the slender stilts for the long run ahead.

Should a hunter for carrying his dream in a big bag to the bush
brag about game that is now a porcupine and soon an ancestor?

Is the masquerade the deity he masks in costume and dance?
Must Mami Wata's* favourite take for granted her python guard?

If they pick up the minstrel's songs in Yaoundé and Gaborone,
have the people heeded the message he bears for the muse;

have Lagos and Abuja abandoned their lascivious ways;
have they challenged the future with the truth of the past?

Have the minstrel's songs translated the unwritten alphabet
into a new lingua franca of perennial love and friendship;

have the songs married north and south and west and east
into one commonwealth not consumed by ethnic rancour?

---

* Mami Wata: mermaid

11

If they sing his songs at Abraka, Accra, and Yerwa,
has he kept the commandments of the providing muse?

In its festive gyrations the sportive kite
should not take its fortune for granted—

in its total abandon to the spirit of that hour,
it can crash and succumb to smoke and fire!

The minstrel smiles, swaggers, and glows,
but let him obey the commandments of the muse—

let the masquerade never claim the divinity
of the god he masks in costume and dance.

The minstrel's livery

And the minstrel must maintain the sanctity
of the costume that he swore to keep clean.

If it ever becomes crushing, he must never
allow it to weigh him down and be soiled;

rather he must spring in it like Okonkwo[*]
and avert the obscene snipes of keen cynics.

If someday the costume becomes feathery,
he must not fly a children's kite in the air

but must carry himself high in chiefly steps
and leave pedestrian rush to vagabond feet.

Since he is everybody in just one body,
he must separate poacher from guard;

he must make a difference by saving truth
from the mauling claws of ferocious lies.

If an elephant, he must tread lightly
and not throw his weight over ants;

if an ant blessed with potency of poison,
he must only sting others in self-defence;

if a crocodile that carries harpooning jaws,
he must not impale any of the fish neighbours.

---

[*] Okonkwo: protagonist in Chinua Achebe's *Things Fall Apart*.

The minstrel nurses the flower whose fragrance
hallucinates; still, he must bring it to full bloom.

He must preserve the prestige of the caste
whose costume he wears to procure his needs,

he must keep clean the costume of his kind
that he enjoys wearing and glows on him,

and that means following the dictates
of the muse, procurer of his pain and joy.

The minstrel's honour

Multitudes of poor ones mob me to drain their tears;
they plead with " I am going to be rich someday"

to exorcise the unfortunate fate of their hardship,
believing the minstrel a magician priest of words.

Many sick from state corruption and personal neglect
seek cures in malarial homes with my healing song;

they believe there's nothing he can't do who sings
the river song and remains dry in a thunderstorm.

Others take the trouble to come so far to validate
self-interpreted dreams of love and prosperity

because they choose to be blind to hopeless cases—
waiting for miracles without faith; not working hard.

Neither T-shirt nor skull cap masks the minstrel
from the anonymity of the stranger that I seek.

Many spot me protesting gas flares and oil blowouts,
arrested in Abuja for torching the robbers' capitol.

The livery gives me out at night with firefly twinkles;
some believe I make love with the muse in the moon—

the couple enjoying an eternal honeymoon in a private planet
of star-spangled attendants. They think I do not pine for more.

The confusing nicknames of homeboy and vagabond
matter not to those who seek the minstrel in the songs—

they see him at close quarters in his livery of minstrelsy
and they hold him to his words to make them free and happy;

from a distance spectators swoon at the ivory palace
of words where nobody resides without being contented.

The livery of the caste that I wear
exposes me to proliferating trials,

but what load placed on me by the muse
isn't an honour to carry with songs?

The market is a thronged crossroads

The market is a thronged crossroads;
there, life and death meet to trade articles.

The crossroads is a confused market;
a cortege passes without a dirge—

they ought to ban displaying corpses
in public places; lying in state is a lie.

The festival always a market of colours,
costumed spirits and humans assemble

to dance freely to each other's delight.
Who knows what they like in the other?

Spirits have their likes among the living;
there's a shadow stalking every human.

The spirits are smoking long pipes;
the generators of the rich foul the air.

If a porcupine prances into town or market,
don't shoot a popular ancestor already dead;

let the antelope graze gracefully,
the family yonder come back to life.

The town is one vast market;
the bush is a busy crossroads.

Who lies down for dead looks
for a way out of the quandary;

ears on the ground at the crossroads
will soon find a sure way to safety,

but where is safety for one in a coma—
return to recover or dash ahead to die?

The festival is a full market
and the market a crossroads

with strangers milling everywhere—
love seeks to fill its open house.

What the spirits do is obscene,
they bathe in bottles of palm oil;

what humans do is beyond comprehension—
a witch parachutes from coven into a well.

The crossroads teems with passersby;
heads covered with caps and scarves.

Those going away want to return;
 returning ones want a chance to go back.

After the crossroads there are so many gates;
you need a secret formula to pass through—

either way leads to another market
again full of murmurs but no wares;

they trade life and death there.
The market is a crossroads.

Without a guide

After the crossroads the minstrel looks back—
his guide has performed a disappearing act.

With only his own shadow following beside,
he must take the rest of the long road alone.

Now without a guide the minstrel embarks
on a journey that will test his years of minstrelsy:

he must scald his tongue seeking cool water;
he must taste bitter drafts to find sweetness,

he must bruise his body with briars and cockle burrs
to get to the road that takes to the gateway of joy.

No more will he find fire before he needs it;
no invisible hands taking over toilsome tasks.

No more will the gates open to herald his arrival,
nor the cherry tree wait for him to shower fruits.

He must personally roast or boil the yam he grows to eat;
no "Food is ready!" or a laid-out table to select his fill.

If those who sing his songs run to him, he must stand
and bear their standard in ongoing battles of self-defence;

if they cry to him after midnight, he must jump from bed
and not whine about separation from his partner's warmth.

Now that he has passed familiar land and the crossroads,
he must saunter ahead; himself his own guide and shield.

Now if he fears, he must not suffer tremors in daylight
but only at night in bed alone can he cry to himself—

the bruises he bears he covers with a broad swath of smiles;
the losses he incurs he counts not to more than recoup them.

If he becomes indigent, he must not be involved in a scam;
rather he must make love with abject want in contentment.

Now without a guide the minstrel sallies forth,
wearing the livery of his caste; the carrier-sacrifice.

The minstrel comes to a river

The minstrel's road staggers into a deep river.
So abrupt the turn, he almost tumbles into water.

If he waits, night will throw its thick net over him
and he knows the ogre he must conquer to go through.

The river is a swirling water snake whose shocks
make a simple mishap in the crossing a mortal crisis.

If he puts behind this river that already leers at him,
he still has six more to cross to claim victory over rivals—

he will then consort with spirits that dance to drumming
and transcend the divide that separates fear from feasting.

The minstrel must go through water before arriving
without tears at the distant land of light and safety.

The flames of night burn without respect for frontiers;
the traveller must impale night with bristling courage.

Those not wearing the livery of sacrifice hurry past;
they disappear stepping into water and reappear

at the other bank; they beckon the watching minstrel
to step into the river and dissolve like a clump of salt.

The minstrel invokes the muse with his flute;
the muse, always awake, waits to be summoned.

The minstrel now sings the deep river song,
and from nowhere a ferry appears for crossing.

A river does not end the minstrel's journey;
it halts him to muse on land and water

until he realises that all he has is only song.
The minstrel meets a river, dreads nightfall.

The minstrel is a fisherman

Wearing the thick mantle of darkness, without
breakfast he sets out long before day breaks
to win spirited dawn's dew-soaked fortune.
The fisherman obeys the frantic call of waters.

With hope of relieving wraiths of fatal hunger,
he boats alone in the herb-dark waters of the delta
where ferocious currents take orders from above;
he is outnumbered by the population underwater.

He holds to his gourd as a wand to use back home.
He knows where famished fish make their refuge;
from experience of living on water he knows that
the big captive fish struggles to be free before dawn.

He steers down the moonless night to the seashore
to throw his net over the waterborne crowd of fins;
learning from the haul of past seasons, he covers
himself with rainfall that often keeps them gullible.

Tell the fisherman adrift that he knows no fear—
he just can't hide from fear with his hooks and net;
what he fears has nothing to do with fish or water.
To do him favour Mammy Water must drag him down.

The python the water queen wears kills out of jealousy;
it must first be won over before embracing timeless beauty—
the bodyguard must be an ally to win her divine blessing.
Without guard the queen of fortune would be slut or slave.

The fisherman knows poachers have yet to catch tadpoles—
the law will catch up with them before the season runs out
and overturns their catch into water for the next cycle
of generations to live through hard times and still prosper.

Back on land from another world, he is suspended on
a spider's web where he acknowledges praises of his love.
And to everyone in the land seized by paroxysms of hunger,
he offers bones that turn into biscuits in impatient mouths.

The minstrel harps at the beach of Negril

The minstrel that carries a bell also carries a harp.
He plucks the harp and cares not who is listening.

He plays music to close the gaps of absence.
He fills solitude with notes of remembrance.

Now the harp plucks itself, serenades a name
he tries hard to put behind his bedroom walls.

The harp rings the name he thought he could
bury in beach sand and least worry about.

The minstrel pays the price of minstrelsy
with the harp that compels from his hands

notes that send him flushing in an assembly,
notes that never fade away from his presence.

He knows what is buried in beach sand lives—
the persistent waves will surely wash it out.

The minstrel that carries a bell to the market
now carries a harp along the beach of Negril.*

To strangers the crazy performance is nothing strange
amidst those begging for tips without uttering a word,

but he is treating a deep wound nobody sees;
putting out fire burning his flesh and bones.

---

* Negril: coastal town that is a tourist centre in Jamaica.

The minstrel is waving a white flag in the open air,
but the conqueror cannot swim across the Atlantic

to claim victory over the barbarian lord of songs;
the victor is blinded by the orange blaze of sunset.

The minstrel takes no water ride to the black cliffs
that gave the Portuguese name to the onshore city,

nor does he wear goggles of deep divers for the fun
of one who came from afar to see corals underwater.

The happy harp possesses his hands; both frenzied.
The sun rises and sinks into the deeps with his harp

that at midnight comes from nowhere to him to pluck
or have no rest from the hapless company of insomnia.

O harp that torments more than the face
on the far side of the Atlantic monster,

do my notes get there to inflict reciprocal madness?
Do I play this harp to pamper tourists I don't know?

The minstrel that takes a bell to the market
carries a harp and fills the beach and walk

with the cry of anguish he must bear until
he returns to make a long-awaited declaration.

I knew you were pregnant

(for Mbwidiffu)

I knew you were pregnant
long before the moon told you the fact;

indeed you were for so long pregnant
without knowing your changed condition—

the infectious warmth that caught me;
a ripeness the cherry fruit would flaunt.

From a distance I saw the pregnancy
before you knew what you carried simply

without knowing was so cherished;
you did not need to wear Saudi gold.

There's been a soft glow on your face
for as long as I can remember knowing you;

there's been so much texture in every word
that you want to hold back but which flies out

and in the air becomes a flaming flower whose
jasmine fragrance Gucci seeks for a secret deal.

I saw the pregnancy in your unhappy moments
when for no reason you swore you were hurt

and wanted no company to excoriate your wound
that bled profusely for you to paint the uneven world—

you would spare the roaches but not the vultures;
you would save slaves and execute their lords.

I caught you dancing naked before a clean mirror
that you did not care to look at for fear of your face

that harboured eyes of Queen Amina* and hair black
but covered that made you a spirited matriarch.

How always so filled and yet hungry—a demanding
deity sure of the fortunate devotee's faith and worship!

I saw your pregnancy while you were in flight
from the circumcising ritual of the maidens—

it flashed in the savannah darkness swathing you,
kept generous djinns as invisible guides and guards.

You carried the pregnancy despite the sad faces
of your sisters to whom sex is a mere suppository.

Long before you dreamed of kissing a lonely night,
I knew you were months and months pregnant

in the rage against broken vows and parents
who called you names before your married friends.

I knew you were already pregnant
when you were washed ashore listening

to the minstrel's magic harp in moonlight
and soon joined the muse to sing blues.

I knew you had carried pregnancy for years
because patience is your unknown but real name;

you watched the commonwealth racked pale,
then invoked thunder to smite politicians

---

* Queen Amina: powerful woman who once ruled Zaria, a Hausa emirate in northern Nigeria.

and in the revolution you dread but love
deliver a woman president to the nation.

I knew you could only be pregnant
in the deep songs you always sing.

For Mbwidiffu

I hear the agonizing cries of girls
in flight from the flashing razor;

I hear horrific howls of daughters
against their parent-sanctioned rape.

Who wants to be held down to wear the stigma
of adult life, her ecstasy wrapped in a rag?

Who wants her yams scorched before harvest,
stripped of womanly pride for old times' sake?

"And they have the nerves to cry out,"
the patriarchs wonder in male-only joints;

"after all, their mothers went through this
without crying or complaining of cruelty!"

These men do not count the army of divorcees—
leaking women no man wants in the neighbourhood;

they look down on their children's wrinkled mothers
morose and up to the neck in forced misery; wrecked.

Of course, the contented men take no count
of the multitude of brides dying at childbirth.

The girls fleeing, the old men complain,
have turned into animals without names.

There's no laughter in the girls that fall in line—
firebrands wipe out sunshine from their faces.

I still hear the chilling wails of the fugitive girls,
the benumbing silence of their ghostly presence

and now the goateed men ask the Maker why these girls
aren't made of the same stuff as their tamed mothers.

The simple answer: "Time has changed!
Time has changed! Time has since changed!"

The muse sends me to the market

I ask no questions of the divine command
and off I go to Igbudu Market* across the main road.

I take along the cast-iron bell that completes my costume—
the messenger must deliver his message with a clear ring.

Above haggling murmurs of milling marketers
I come to mingle with sellers, buyers, and others.

The market is a vast theatre of fortune where
fate tags its caste with myriad sizes of purses:

those come with only a penny to buy all their needs
and a few with tons of cash to buy what is not for sale.

It is clear the divides elsewhere that remain covered
the market surely exposes in abysmal barriers.

Forbidden love exercises freedom here; nobody denied entry
where the living and the dead consort and exchange pleasantries

under the shade of thronged murmurs, spectacle of spices
and stalking robbers display their learned tortoise's craft.

I have not come to the market on my own volition
to barter songs for palm oil, fresh fish, or table salt—

the songs that come free to the minstrel will not
outbid the oil worker's wife overflowing with cash.

---

* Igbudu Market: a big market by the Warri-Sapele Road in Warri.

I come to poeticize the arithmetic of prices,
denials of poverty and delusions of wealth.

I ring the bell at tilted scales and other measures;
I sing loud against the hat tricks of usurers.

The muse sends me to the market,
and I ask no questions of the divine command.

The minstrel is a refugee

Before he realises it,
the minstrel is a refugee

without even a pen in the pocket for possession;
with neither minutes nor paper to scribble the blues

he must sing to carry along the memory
of the shrew that battered him into flight.

Every property too ponderous to carry,
the refugee must travel light in flight—

it is only life that he carries simply with-
out knowing its significance that counts.

The minstrel in a black Indian file
evacuates the death-taunting city—

he has jumped from the roof into a boat;
no stunt that saves life is ever strange.

The minstrel seeks refuge in the kingdom
where the house of words cannot flatten

from the mindless cruelty of Katrina;*
much in the head cannot be trashed.

The muse hits the minstrel with a hurricane,
teaches the primitive lessons of a cyber age—

---

* Katrina: hurricane that devastated New Orleans in September 2005.

the common denominator of survival for all
surpasses whatever bank accounts or stardom.

From murderous Katrina's fury he flees;
the minstrel fears death by drowning

hence he looks not back at the gorgon's face
to gather valuables and be transfixed into stone.

The minstrel counts the blessings of a fugitive;
the muse that subjects the caste to calamities

also saves from the road littered with aborted hopes
and makes the favourite one to defy odds to survive.

The song though invaluable is no property that
drowns—even if it goes down, it rises with life;

the song survives unsanitary domes of starvation;
it survives the neglect of smug federal bureaucrats.

The minstrel takes his gruel scrambled from filth
and seeks not the king's table on a flooded floor;

he wishes to arrive sane with memories of Katrina,
his head clean above the muck; no personal tragedy.

The horizon once an insurmountable wall
beckons with clouds that give way to sun,

and always stalking the minstrel
a beautiful spirit, lips aflame—

the wordless delight springs from pain;
the companion thinks of labour's fruits.

The minstrel wails

(in memory of Ezenwa-Ohaeto)

At last death threw you down flat
after you wrestled with all your warrior heart.

Until the final fall even with deep bruises,
brave one, your face still lit with smiles.

Death that tackled the elephant to fall in the forest,
who can escape its stifling grasp in a clearing?

Why it picked on you so early, I know not.
We are all prone to the random punch of woes.

Mine is to wail the sapling iroko struck by lightning.
The minstrel's voice stilled but swathed with songs.

It is not the elder's beat to lead the wail for the young
and you were not even age-mate in the calendar of birth

but o Muse, suspend the rules of rituals
for a fellow minstrel muted in high noon.

Wandering minstrel, you traversed the world with songs.
Sojourner, you made home of every known soil.

A minstrel leaves and the living ones muse—
the young elephant falls and the forlorn family wails.

We cannot tell the mind of fate—who receives
the blessings of minstrelsy suffers its calamitous blow.

The muse that lavishes her favourite with gifts,
the same muse gives him up in a storm to spirits.

36

You who brought firewood to the communal hearth,
  stoked it and kept warm everybody in the cold,

you who placed your harvest of yams on the table
so that no one would be tortured by furious famine,

you made a road to the sun and to the moon
so that there will always be pathways to our dreams

but fate knocked down the reflective signs you set up
in its forays to draw sadness from your happy songs.

You wanted to be president to share pumpkins to people,
your song of a soldier routed coup-makers from barracks;

you knew the chant of the night masquerade
and feared not the guttural tirades in the dark.

You were minstrel of all seasons and peoples
and no hand could cover the brilliance of your sun.

The commander of songs falls in the battlefield,
foot-soldiers take over the standard fighting on.

Death tackles the young elephant to a fall,
but the tusks raise songs that outlive the call—

we lose what we love and live on with the virtues;
so your voice reverberates with ardour from beyond.

The wail for the startling star covered by dust-clouds
must stop; the beauty of appearance lives on with us

for another dawn in the making—you live everywhere,
and the living must stop wailing for the new life

that gives the departed another lease of life
to bloom beyond the fatalities of poachers.

Today

Today the muse trashes my craft,
and that's not all I suffer in one day.

The sun turns my bird's motley feathers into soot;
smoke from the rejected offering suffocates.

The moon lives in the room in a blindfold,
the stars gone to hide from their bride.

The garden one bush flower whose blazing
petals poison eyesight with poor perception.

I am looking for a fruit in the wilds
that will purge me clean of daydream.

The day has laid siege to my hope;
my faith suffocates in a cell of lust.

Today the muse offers me manna
laced all over with shreds of misery.

The eagle's feathers grey in numbers,
the iroko's crown struck by lightning.

On earth paradise is a daydream;
dream must give way to wakeful life.

I no longer ask where the bird is flying;
freedom is a birthright of fugitives.

The distance between the minstrel and the muse
cannot be contracted by a spell alone;

songs of absence cannot cover the void
into which the cherished hope has slipped.

Today the muse smacks the minstrel;
life must take over from daydream—

the lie of paradise the truth of hell;
the flower of feathers flaming soot.

Rigours of absence break the beauty's resolve,
tears flow through the telephone line.

The muse mocks the minstrel;
moon and stars abandon night.

The mermaid left a snake on land,
the hallowed queen slipped into water;

the mermaid returns with her spell underwater,
the minstrel on his own cannot live with her wonder.

The flower of the heart's nursery a wreath
tossed into waves after her disappearing act;

the muse throws the minstrel into a rack.
Nobody cares about the pain of the gift.

The house of words is paradise of pain;
the kingdom of songs the throne of throes.

The muse that paves the road closes passageways,
the flower that hallucinates also lacerates the heart.

The mermaid invited the minstrel to her court;
a snake pinned him down in the bedchamber.

Today the minstrel turns away from his avid mocker,
smiles over wounds and shuns the plethora of stabs.

The muse has smacked the minstrel with a thunderbolt,
and today life takes over from hallucinating daydream.

The minstrel tells tales

I

I asked Mami Wata[*] to teach me how to swim.
I ended up not knowing how to swim to safety—

a drowned man; a prisoner in her palace of coral
and weeds. She blows big bubbles into the air,

and I am the trophy decking her proud dominion.
Don't ask who drowns not to teach you to swim.

II

The moon basks on the polished beach sand.
I watch waves wash and kiss her feet.

The lone beauty radiates white light;
around her resplendence of divine fire.

I immerse my body in her splendour;
I do not seek freedom from love.

I have summoned the queen out of court;
she has kept me wakeful in the savannah night.

---

[*] Mami Wata: mermaid, and currently used to designate goddess of beauty and fortune.

The minstrel looks toward dawn

They gather armies of lust to overwhelm him.
They close all gates with a deathwatch,

but he takes a chance at roads that have
no directions but run smoothly on. . .

Will gunshots bring peace to the troubled land?
The jobless enlist in the army of brutes.

Unpaid workers watch their families break;
no divine message breaks through Aso Rock.

The song of the returning minstrel floats
above cacophonies of gunshots and brawls.

The minstrel's voice alone on the road,
does he rally folks or start a stampede?

He heads for where refugees are pouring out,
sings to find the way to a hospitable state.

Alone he wanders humming faithfully
the forgotten anthem of national salvation.

It is still dark since there's been no dawn.
He sings lonely of a dawn that defies imagining.

The road littered with mangled hopes,
can he defy odds to enter the city at dawn?

A drought of dust infects eyes and there
 a visionless gaze before abysmal depths,

but the poetry of the day leads the minstrel on
to capture the totem pet and release it into dawn.

Self-portrait

I

Let others occupy walled mansions,
I live in the open house of words.

They seek fulfilment in the river,
I court the sea to satisfy my yearnings.

They school in showers,
I graduate in a hurricane.

They are easily filled;
voluptuous is my appetite.

II

I am a river
journeying seaward,

blind to my fate.
Will the sea I seek

for all its fortune
shed a tear-drop

should mountain
or woodland

that I trespass
cut me off?

III

The minstrel looks to the underwater lounge
of the muse for refuge, but on land

he frantically waves a firebrand
at the gaunt limbs of drought-stricken plants;

he summons the god of mischief
to give a command performance

of all days that he is so hungry
he wants to show the combustible side of power.

Spectators, roll up your sleeves—Houdini's
surprises are predictable; not this.

Tomorrow is too deep to fathom—
will today's seeds germinate or die?

May the thunderstorm rumbling overhead
pre-empt the unguarded blaze

from consuming fresh and dry leaves!
The devotee invokes the avenger

without first feeding him blood of sacrifice
to douse his flaming appetite.

The minstrel looks to the underwater lounge
of the water-maid for refuge, but on land

he knows not the limits he has crossed.
The rumbling thunderstorm brings relieving news.

IV

The minstrel suffers the bite of his words;
a caste founded on love carries so much pain.

Words ambush him whichever road he takes;
sometimes his own words rail against him

and those wearing his livery of songs are first
to cry revolution and threaten with neck-lacing.

He must not take for granted their humble origins,
armed with the warrior spirit that yields to no one.

Living in the house of words and obeying rules of the caste
do not cover him from the mean menace of insults,

but when he is mocked he feels no shame
in the pain that is not different from love.

He carries words as clubs, bullets for self-defence,
flowers, whose petals he throws at his idol's feet.

The loan

(remembering my father, after the traditional festival)

One cannot invest a loan in a brighter project.
I am not one praising a borrower for his debts,

but you are a hero. The spectacle of four loud days
of cannon has changed your life into a blazing star.

The world lived with a victor without knowing him.
You carried an elephant on the head and still danced.

The debtor is damned; you are the people's saviour.
The world owes you salvoes of gratitude for your craft.

The borrower meets disgrace; you are everybody's
darling, proudly pointed at as model of your group.

You wanted to make a big splash in the festival,
took a loan from the rich to buy tons of gunpowder.

You, without a penny but thinking so big, came first;
you have amassed a wealth nobody around can surpass.

The spectators witnessed the magic you pulled out of nothing;
the orators are still inventing superlatives to compliment you.

"This festival comes only once in twenty-something years,"
you said, "and time ahead is always an asset to the living."

To outsiders you are next to the king, a prince.
You stole the show from loudmouthed chiefs—

to the townsfolk you are the fortunate one;
your gunshots reported loudest in every ear.

The commoner that looks far ahead becomes a chief,
the daring hunter that downs the leopard keeps its skull;

the chameleon wins the contest of primary colours,
wears a rainbow out beside others in suits of soot.

It's politics defeating others in their invented games;
the tortoise wins the tortuous contest of guile and wiles.

The world knows that who hurled out thunderbolts
to wake and cheer up gods in agony cannot be indigent.

What dancer can be summoned to out-dance the grub
whose every movement of life is itself a sweet dance?

Champion before every searching eye of doubters,
the meteor burns itself out to make a noble gesture

for which the world brands itself with fire
to cultivate memories to outlive the crash.

You have won hearts of beauties and drummers;
you have seen joy, taken home trophies of glory.

After this you can throw yourself to sweat it out
to assuage the hurt hearts of your jealous creditors.

Let those who had the means and held back lament,
let them wait for another twenty years to challenge you—

then the glory you wear will have grown smarter
and the world and gods know only one favourite.

Stardom

There is a stark transparency in dark things:
night lights up the moon and stars to see with.

At the tale's end, the beginning is obvious:
the echo reports a nearby voice from far away.

Every aspect of geography falls into a map;
there's room for aliens to be hosted in the globe.

In the riverbank, mud has custody of diamonds;
for once servants hold captive their terrible lord.

A vision blinds the minstrel to celebrate with songs—
beyond the void swallowing others, he sees stardom.

Highland dreams

At this castle height deep in Caledonian country,[*]
night is so light that sleep dreams out its short portion.

Last night I chopped down trees of centuries
and gathered animals and birds into a cage.

I renamed the survivor population of captives
with sectarian appellations imported from a dead country—

friendly ghosts applauded for the adventurous spirit
and I was knighted by the vassal lord of conquest.

If that were all, the world would be the same;
the sane would wish to wander round and see

what new outfit would cover their nakedness;
but we know the distance it took to come this far.

A new tribe of trees popped up with waterproof bands
round their wrists—all wanted to be chronicled victims.

There wasn't much else to do with the birds that lost wings;
I, dressed in a feather hat, decorated before being dethroned.

My community wins the right to live without fear
and draws up a charter empowering daydreamers

to overtake fugitives before dusk, mend broken bones
that are the bane of those prone to falling on rocks.

And behold Mungo Park[+] carrying a map that is
a charter of highland dreams, looking for the Niger

---

[*] at Hawthornden Castle, near Edinburgh, Scotland. June 9, 2004.

[+] Mungo Park: Scotsman who claimed to have discovered the River Niger, where people had always lived for centuries in West Africa.

and his poor porters pointing to the great river;
now camped to be fed on fish they had caught!

At this castle height deep in Caledonian country,
night is so light that sleep dreams out its short portion.

Waiting

The elders advise us to wait till we grow old;
wow, wait for their privileges till we are told.

The politicians tell us to wait till their second term;
hurray, wait for prosperity till after we re-elect them.

The dreamers teach us to watch till they wake;
yes, wait till they make it to another daybreak.

They always ask us to keep on waiting all the time;
yes, learn from them to wait out an entire lifetime.

Think again

I will think again.

The chief priest of the *Awoshi* cult[*] converted into
the Deeper Life Church that burned down his shrine.

I will think again.

He who left by car since morning for the market had
not got there when I arrived on foot in the afternoon.

I will think again.

It clouded and threatened to storm in the east all day
but it is in the west where it was clear that it now pours.

I will think again.

The doctor of paediatrics that the world flocks to
failed to save his son from dying of convulsion.

I will think again.

The jury of rivals I protested against
awarded me our coveted love.

I will think again.

Sunbird, you sang persistently for rain
and now you are drowning in the deluge.

Think again.

---

[*] Awoshi: cult of the 1950s in the Urhobo area of Delta State whose members made sacrifices of
chickens to their god.

Alligator choices

The alligator leaves water
for a taste of life on land,

exchanges a wet dominion
for a foothold of brushes,

leaves fin-spluttering music
for a choir of reed-tuned birds.

It wants to stay as long as it pleases
to stretch itself and bask in the sun's

open country, ensconced among
shrubs that scratch its craggy back.

It wants to forage for the food
that will fill its patience with joy,

and, in tearful satisfaction, celebrate
a beautiful life out of the mainstream.

Comes a thunderstorm and in a flash
it scuttles back into water, back to where

it fled a while ago for the refuge
that so easily splinters in lightning.

A storm pours water and the alligator
knows it is capable of a deluged sheet,

but that is neither a river nor a lake.
The sun is not its permanent residence,

and over the exposed country of luxuries
that attracts with prospects of paradise,

over the provisional delight
that blinds starkly in thunder,

it chooses the familiar home of water
to safely exercise its maximum power.

Supreme artist

Wandering in dust-laden Mararaba,[*]
amidst roaring traffic and mad crossings,
seeking Gordon's Spark[+] to fill the night,
a Plateau-accented voice hits me from afar;

a young man serenading the restless night,
hugging a pretty-contoured harp. I run after
the musician for some distance, catch up
with the divine voice of a vulgar evening.

He sings and plays the harp so beautifully,
I am enthralled; we stand by the roadside.
Brighter than ever, moon and stars dazed
beside the astral-cued chords in his hands.

I draw him a safe distance from the road
to fill me with draughts of what he plucks,
and there for a quarter hour entertains me.
The world stands still as he plucks on and on.

I ask what it will take to get such a harp.
"This one I specifically made for myself."
And he plays "Jesus is coming for the righteous."
Enraptured, I want to hold to his voice and harp.

He says he can make another harp for me
and I ask for his home, which he describes—
behind Aso School. He points to a welder:
"Ask for his friend playing his self-strung harp."

---

[*] Mararaba: a town on the Abuja-Jos Road in Nasarawa State, Nigeria.
[+] Gordon's Spark: a mildly alcoholic drink.

54

A week in Mararaba and I meet a supreme artist
so enchanted by his harp and singing with his whole
body that I seek him out to make one for me. And his
voice and rhythm follow me from that sparking night.

Bonfire

It started with a thunderous aplomb—
a fuel-doused exclamation of flames!

It grew wilder and soon smoke disappeared
for smoulders to exercise their festive display.

The sparks competed with a full constellation of stars,
and the world kept silent listening to the blazing laughter.

Thanks to mystic Stephen who provided multiple trucks
of deadwood that fed the flames into delirious frenzy.

Sitting before the fire soothingly warm on a late August night,
gazing at the glowing face of the fire, we imagined death by fire

but our minds turned with the wind to the origin of bonfires—
roasting venison to celebrate fresh victory after battle.

Artists fight their battle with a vision of perfection
(the beauty of the gazelle, dewdrops on grass at full moon)

that often eludes them until set on paper, canvas, or performed.
There is so much stored in the mind that cannot go up in flames.

We relished memories of primitive pleasures
that simple ones took for granted in caves.

The women watched the flames for a while and withdrew
with a map of the constellations to call stars by their names,

and they summoned the spirits of as many as they could.
I thought of the Dogons with a thousand names for stars.

At Steepletop the stars are not constant companions,
but tonight they brandish their sparkling faces

and the sparks leaping, gyrating in formations, now gentle
then wild, tell a fireside tale of a gathering of artists

talking about sex and other private matters in muted tones
not to interfere with the laughter of companion spirits.

How many times is the world at peace and celebrating?
Not often do the stars and sparks team up to delight warriors.

Durban

(on the occasion of Poetry Africa 2005)

Fabled land of Shaka* that yields to no one,
your *imbongi*+ voice reverberates across Africa.

Your soil carries a current that fortifies my soles;
your ocean-flushed air fills me with youthful zest.

In your soil the stump grows back into a stout trunk.
Your entire landscape glows with a proud heritage.

I invoke your warrior spirit of centuries
to reinforce my ancestral vigilance.

Without guard, freedom can slip away;
without vision, fortune can fritter into nothing.

Without memory, the trail will be lost
to the life-sustaining springs of famished times.

You brandished the assegai to keep your own—
the giant's presence protects the entire neighbourhood.

I invoke your warrior spirit of centuries
to reinforce my ancestral vigilance.

In the streets the beads and fabrics that costume you
into only one of a majestic kind worldwide.

The elephant only brings forth a big offspring—
sons and daughters of the lightning spear stand upright.

Beauty garments the mountains, plains, and veldts
into one body whose spectacle takes the breath away.

---

* Shaka: the emperor who built the Zulu nation in South Africa.

+ imbongi: Zulu poet who chants poetry spontaneously.

I invoke your warrior spirit of centuries
to reinforce my ancestral vigilance.

You no longer tiptoe in your own land.
You stride with the majesty of the giraffe.

Ama-Zulu, who does not know that you
people not only the earth but also the heavens?

Who attempts to hold you down (and many
tried it with regret) thrusts his hands into fire.

I invoke your warrior spirit of centuries
to reinforce my ancestral vigilance.

In the kingdom of songs we share one standard:
you praise as I abuse; both necessities of life.

In the house of words we speak the same lingua franca
of love but will not allow guests to seize our inheritance.

One smears a rival, but I revere you.
One pulls down a challenger, but I raise you to the sun.

I invoke your warrior spirit of centuries
to reinforce my ancestral vigilance.

We, scions of the same sturdy loins,
our bloods coalesce into an invincible force;

our birthrights surpass others' measures of wealth;
our thundering chants drown the roar of lions.

In Durban the dark shadow dissolves into a warm-hearted host
and all languages of the world become one human song.

I invoke your warrior spirit of centuries
to reinforce my ancestral vigilance.

The minstrel lives a homeboy

The minstrel lives a homeboy outside his nativity,
driven homeward by an exotic spirit he embraces

and with whom he breathes healing draughts
into the body racked by persistent civil strife.

He reinvents native songs in foreign lands
and returns to sing them to audiences

that for long yearned for their lost voice
now swathed in a novel ring of their pride.

He wears on his bare chest a *pro unitate* badge
that opens hospitable doors across the country.

The minstrel lives outside his home state
where words are flowers that he croons

to gather to adorn his cherished landscape
for the beauty that he knows captivates all.

He finds outside comfortable and there
cultivates the native beauty of utterances

that the muse flips at him from the nursery
that none reaches without falling in adoration.

Where the minstrel lives he adorns with all
he can imagine from the variegated garden.

At the taxi station

A bible-brandishing man suddenly appears from nowhere
once the car is filled with passengers and about to leave

to pray for the passengers before the car takes off
for its six-hour dust-coated destination of discomfort.

He rails against demons—not the potholed bush-covered roads;
he rails against accidents—not drowsy or drunk illiterate drivers.

He wants the road cleared by the blood of Christ—not Works;*
he absolves robbers from the road—not from unemployment.

The pastor asks the travellers to close their eyes, which they do
even as his remain wide open, and winces at the rebel minstrel

and invokes Christ to cover the car that is often not serviced
with the miraculous blood of Jesus; he separates one into two.

He expels all principalities that will lurk along the way
that the overloaded and crowded car will speed past;

he delivers every passenger into the safe hands of God
even as the impatient driver readies bribes for the police.

The holy one summons Christ from above to be the driver
since the paid uniformed one will fall asleep from revelry

and on and on until he concludes with "In the mighty name
of Jesus" to which his congregation on wheels choruses "Amen!"

---

* Works: Ministry of Works.

"The Lord blesses a cheerful giver," he proclaims as he pulls
off his sleeves all the beggar skills he certainly thrives on

and his eyes roving from one traveller to another for his service,
many tuck naira notes onto his outstretched right palm

and, cheered by the generosity, beams a sunflower of smiles
and proclaims "Go well!" as the driver pulls out of the station

with passengers who want to get to their destination
by other means than the transport fare they had paid.

Bonny

I

The island will assuage the hurt of the denial of water
that has broken his peace, the minstrel intuitively believes

as he sets out in the company of his old love for Bonny,[*]
the modern crossroads where the fire of sacrifice blazes

and native and newcomer workers carouse in the affluence
that is the persistent debate in faraway houses of assembly.

I imagine a horse riding me through waves to the island,
I foresee the queen's burnished throne burning out the night.

I see without looking at the riches of the sea placed in the sun;
I hear from no voices the thrilling song awaiting the pilgrim.

This island will surely assuage the passion of three decades
that rioted without stop to possess and dethrone the prince

from the lofty plateau where rock-rooted plants flourish.
The water-swathed body must glisten with beauty, he thinks.

But thought is only a garland of wishes worn without fuss,
its logical end may falter before the day's gone in a flash.

In the dream the island is filled with boats of fishermen
and a regatta entertains the seated beards from outside.

When mist falls off the face of the crowded island,
the queen abdicates her throne of gold for deep water;

---

[*] Bonny: island town of Nigeria's Rivers State that is an oil centre.

the streets are then flooded with fortune of the season
that drowns sun and moon in every camp of fishers.

From the beginning the island holds captive desires
that keep the minstrel a devotee of the water sect

and, in plunging into water to resurface onto land,
he holds his breath before inhaling salt and brine.

II

The roaring flames are no sacrificial bonfires,
not the annual congress of devotees and their pantheon;

the thundering blaze is not a series of festival cannons
to serenade providers of communal plenty, health and happiness.

No more the divine bounty all year round to brag about;
it all went up in incessant gas flares and oil blowouts.

Once so rich in water resources songs praised
the proverbial magnanimity of the water goddess

but no more the hilarity of humans at home;
only cornucopia of woeful tears, lamentations

for the fires that consume the evergreens
and cascades of grease that clog prided wetlands.

No more within reach the fish for the next meal,
nor the fruits falling from ripeness of the season.

III

The minstrel is an island populated
by natives and immigrants living on one another.

The island is a dialogue of tender words,
a congress of birds, fish, flowers and flares.

I conquered fear of drowning in the island;
the earth resists the assault of the waves.

I left Bonny happy; laughter muffled wails.
The island grew big in the thirty-year dream

and Bonny still lives above water,
swathed in inevitable water and fire.

The minstrel's school

The minstrel is building a school whose subjects
will be rivers, evergreens, and aviaries;

an institute of health and happiness
that will guard against all kinds of poachers.

The students will hug one another
in a classroom of steaming love

in a relationship that so pounds the heart
that they will be ready to die to keep each other alive.

The teachers will be the beauties of the land—
simple-costumed animals, fishes, and birds;

they know so well the soil, water, and air
that the community relies on to live free.

The classes will hold under sun or rain
in ponds, farms, and moonlit playgrounds.

The graduates will be missionaries of a revived faith
that feel as much for every other life as their own;

they will clasp themselves in a long chain
that makes one life part of all life—

in the land the anthem of coexistence will ring
happy notes that will be everyone's duty to sing.

The minstrel is building an open school for all
with the natural resources at his disposal,

and he is sure the experiment will work so well that
from everywhere will come people to fill the school.

The beauty I have seen

The beauty I have seen in abundance abroad,
no picture however embellished can capture;

the stars that have shone their hearts for me,
the same brilliance they can never replicate for the world.

I know why Akpalu[*] brags about the Hausa picking up
his Ewe songs; his heart beats an ecstatic drum—

the homeboy freezes the thousand witnesses
that saw his coronation as chieftain of songs.

Who will find the remains of that day and know
what spell the spectacle held for the thronging eyes?

The lucent face beaming smiles to the packed ballroom
salutes Aridon,[+] the divine mentor, for the gift of words;

nobody can be richer than the fortunate minstrel whose
every gesture of a grand masquerade receives applause.

Not often do so many gods convene in conclave
for this spectacle they brighten with their smiles.

The cannonade has rolled over mountain and valley
and the muse has given a nod to the minstrel—

the ululations that rock the stars enter the echoes
that bridge far and near in transmuted songs.

---

[*] Akpalu: famous Ghanaian Ewe oral poet who sang songs of sorrow.
[+] Aridon , god of memory of Nigeria's Urhobo people; also muse.

How can the minstrel display the effervescence
of the present to outlive the very moment that blooms?

The magic pageant has won the day,
let the minstrel put the gift into song—

memory nudges on with its constellations
but that beauty's hour can't relive its prime.

The beauty I have seen in its fullest radiance,
no picture however embellished can capture.

The muse won't let me quit

Even if I wanted, Aridon wouldn't
leave me alone—the tasks of the caste

cannot be cast away by the minstrel at will;
minstrelsy I now know is a lifelong path.

Sometimes you are everybody's envy, applauded
at home and abroad; heart lifted out of the world.

At other times the tribulations too crushing,
the minstrel cries in bed from the burden he bears.

Even if I vow to lay down the costume,
Aridon won't let me quit the caste of my life.

For the shame of losing his most ardent worshiper,
the god of songs will never let me quit.

II

Doors of the Forest
& Other Poems

For:
Kite, also in his special place

We did not only disfigure the forest but flared its seeds,
not only knocked out birds with catapults but poisoned the air;
we cleared the land of what gave us life with their lives.

Doors of the forest

"The doors of the forest are closed" (Pablo Neruda)

The doors of the forest are closed. Forever
closed by poachers, government-salaried guards,
of the green dominion that kissed the sky's face
amidst ululation of leaves topped by a majestic crown.
On the dome and over the garland of opulent leaves,
the choir out-sang symphonies, vocals of every calibre—
soloists, duets, and ensembles pouring out melodies.
The bush was a countryside fair of a thousand voices
that rang from pre-dawn through wakeful hours.

The doors are now closed to the population of *treedom*
after the holocaust of millennial axes and cutlasses;
a vast dune is the brown seat of the imperial desert
with hot air conducting the triumphant trumpet of victors.
Imagine the loss in capital and heritage of the nobility
of the iroko, mahogany, obeche, and the lineage of heights!
All the shields against fearsome diseases trampled to dust.
Once the giants got decapitated, the undergrowths wiped out,
all other species of glamour ground into interminable sand.

With the forest gone, the bloodbath hushed over by rites
of sprinkling confetti at wraiths of a once proud stock;
the doors themselves fuelled the delirium of seasonal fires.
Once the doors of the forest closed, came a new millennium
of woodless silence—a gaping wound in the earth's chest
thrives with worldwide denial of rain to douse flames.
Humans, shut out, smart from the climate change.
The doors of the forest are closed to peace and joy
by the poaching perpetrated in the silence of lust.

I hoped to climb a ladder to the sky

The trees preceded the tribes in the land we call ours.
They foiled fierce floods and dug deep their feet
before the womb that bore us broke its concealed sac.

And the colourful clans of birds arrived early in the wetlands,
dancing on slender reeds that themselves swayed to the wind—
nobody knew where the spirit came from to possess all.

We would have had no homes, no doors and roof overhead,
without the primeval abundance that blessed us, proud ones
believing that we lacked nothing we needed to live well.

We would have been wraiths from the vacuous womb
without the beasts that filled the earth, air, and water;
they groomed us to assume the graceful gait of arrogance.

And when satiated, we forgot wood still mattered;
after stilts that raised us far up brought us safely down
and the sky gods nodded to our sacrificial mounds.

The same way we embarked upon a ritual hunt to ferret out
every life in water, air, and on the soil to pamper appetites
that turned into voracious monsters after we became strong.

Roaring, the desert advances to take over our refuge;
the hot winds landing countless battalions of sand regiments
to swamp crowds of people now captives to inhuman habits.

As for the famine feverishly fanning out to every corner,
it rebukes the hands that slaughtered blindly in the country
now quartered in emaciated bodies doddering everywhere.

As a child, I hoped to climb a ladder to the sky and there
meet the bearded Osonobrughwe* who granted every wish.
I had faith the friendly forest would provide me the craft.

I hoped to be borne on wings, long before aeroplanes
tore through clouds—there was no jet with the majesty
of the *apiapia*+ gliding overhead to assure me of safety.

We did not only disfigure the forest but flared its seeds,
not only knocked out birds with catapults but poisoned the air;
we cleared the land of what gave us life with their lives.

Each of us can only remember rivers in flowing robes,
species of birds or game that now thrive only in memory;
the forest, its doors, and all flared in a foolhardy frenzy.

It's clear what we did to those who preceded us here.
Now we hang by a precipice in place of the paradise.
We have lost it, the beautiful country we were born into.

---

* *Osonobrughwe*: Urhobo for the Supreme God.
+ Urhobo for "Falcon"

Lamentations of the herbalist

I

A stripped landscape boasts of no herbalist in sight.
Lost, the lingua franca of green learned from birth
even though I did not migrate to another country.
The big-hearted forest once provided all my needs,
nursed the herbs with which I performed miracles.
Its evergreen coat stripped by bands of poachers,
arsonists, and a cavalry of prospectors tearing down
trees and trampling the lush carpet of undergrowths.

No longer the presence of the teeming population of
every ethnicity welcoming me to the shaded dominion;
only ghosts of a host population that once thrived here.
There is no solace that the vacuum will be refilled
with whatever new growth has taken over the landscape
and the spoken word will transfuse it into a new cure.
An invading force overwhelmed me and my caste,
shot peppery sand onto the eyes to rob us of vision
and set us in a confused state where lost memory reigns—
blinded eyes' tears cannot bring back roads of the past
that led to draughts to imbibe with words of power.

My dew-wet stretch of goat path is torn open into
a highway for tankers to take oil to inland ports.
I now languish in a desolate land without a name,
robbed of green and its potency, and now my hands
cannot infuse health onto multiplying crowds of patients.
How do I wash away the taints that condemn the sick?
How sharpen the vision of blurred eyes without herbs?
How relieve harrowing headaches of tortured ones?
I am now called by the name of who I used to be,
without tools that I need to invoke gods from high
to bestow health on those I dish out doses of herbs.

II

I remember birds' droppings that fed the dominion,
animal shit that littered ruts that led me like a hunter
to vegetable clusters moistened by the piss of warthogs.
To me grass, weeds, and herbs flourished as neighbours
and from the same soil roots shot out what I sought
to heal patients with primeval ointments of the land.
I remember the forest as one remembers a constant provider
that lost its ability to be generous, stripped of its abundance;
a provider whose life is on the line, heading for inevitable demise.

I remember plucking herbs in the labyrinths of damp trails,
counting in threes, sevens, or nines for necessary efficacy—
I plucked and counted, for numbers made a dosage right.
At dawn or dusk, I paid tributes to the keepers of the forest;
threw coins at all directions that would invite me for my needs
because nothing is free and I paid for what I would take away.
I murmured arcane songs so that healing gods would show
the way to where stood the herbs I wanted among undergrowths,
before night blackened everywhere into a wilderness of shadows.

I remember rain washing clean the herbs before my arrival
or the sun lavishly pouring light on them for my vision.
When it rained and sunned together, the gods in congress,
I knew whatever words I invoked carried divine potency.
In my search, snakes slithered past, poisoning no friendly feet;
petals opened to me the brightness in all cheered by daylight.
From this distance, across the fires of capital, new affluence,
I remember the multi-ethnic population of small ones
for whom I was a provider of proven cures, a blessed healer.
For all that the forest once gave me, I sing this sad song.

On New Year's Eve, 2006

1

Treating a painful but bearable disease with fatal infections
clearing impurities from the street with a mudslide

breaking the stick meant to be bent into a bow
drowning the dirty child in a pool instead of washing him with a
bucket

giving a preordained verdict before the trial's done
burying the sick instead of allowing the patient to go either way

when will the overstretched hands of the callous one
be amputated by the saviour of small ones?

Despite the blindfold the world knows the hangman;
despite our profuse tears, we see the murderer's profile.

2

So the year ends with the harrowing howl of mourners
as perpetrators of their pain celebrate the conquest

so the year ends precisely arranged by imperial gods
as repercussions of their sorties echo worldwide

so the year ends with a brief presidential statement
without acknowledging culpability for the countrywide rubble

so the year ends for the superman as planned
as confusion forces others into shocked silence

so the year ends without the chief judge being sentenced
for the verdict of death to placate his racist god

so the year ends with armed marauders celebrating the New Year
while their victims lie wrapped in white calico

so the year ends without ending our fears and tears
without the death of the monster shackling pious ones

so the year ends with a decomposing corpse
without birth or conception of a beautiful one.

To the Adivasis

(after watching Vinod Raja's *Mahua Memories*)

Water was the blood of the hills, abundant
spring water the gift of the generous gods.

The forest was the perennial provider of foods
with special fruits of plants only that soil knew.

The caves offered solace from tantrums of sun and rain,
and there rites of nativity flourished unknown to strangers.

That was the life they knew from time immemorial,
that was the only cradle of their rooted civilization.

Caterpillars bulldozed serene hills standing majestically,
they inflicted gaping wounds upon the earth.

Then came the explosion of the hills and they lost
the shrines and paintings of their ancestors;

the forests were shamefully stripped naked
and they lost their Providence's kind hands.

They lost their springs, rivers, and lakes;
they lost the life spring of their existence.

Trucks crushed children, men, and women
stopping their fortune from being stolen.

Police and soldiers guarded the looters
and shot at adivasis[*] standing for their rights—

---

[*] adivasi: Indian untouchable or low caste person.

they chose to die rather than see their wealth
they knew was god-given stolen from them;

they stood with their bare bodies as shield
but the poachers had no shred of conscience.

The strangers killed sons and husbands
and funeral pyres blazed day and night.

The brave stood in their homes and lands
and fell rather than live in further shame;

they wielded every power they knew how to muster—
ritually bathed their warriors that still fell from bullets;

their priests invoked all the gods to deliver them
but the monster still devoured them and their land.

The monster now wears pearls excavated from the land;
the Minister of Mines said he knew nothing of the deaths,

the adivasi dirge that woke everybody did not reach Delhi
that closed its ears and eyes to the massacre.

O my forgotten people, o children of the earth,
I sing this song to wipe your profuse tears—

the sun will rise to shed light
on the death of the monster,

the children of the tiger will in the end
reclaim their blood spilt over their homes.

Cemetery of hearts

"In others' hell we made our happiness."
—*Derek Walcott*

Who in the cannon-loud campaign
comes out to condemn the commander
for the carnage that earns him medals?

Neither here nor there the majority
counts in stopping lords of injustice;
awesome force of brutes overcomes

but that is not peace at night, fear-free life.
You cannot vanquish nightmares with
made-up smiles or baby-smashing bombs.

Can one still say gun or bomb is no solution
to the fires consuming the people's pastures,
with prayers and praises loud on so many lips?

Neither raised hands nor thumbprints
of dissent stop drunken cavalier barons
from levelling streets vibrant and beautiful,

and a deluge of fire, spectre of the end,
steals through corners and the dark
on wings to shed blood of the poor.

They go outside to con philanthropy
and rob what they cannot take by wiles.
Though poor we live happier than lords

who, as memory testifies, sacrifice others
to gods without qualms but always calm
for their comfort and power to overcome.

Between the king and his men at arms
on television to counter truth with brazen
lies, yawns a tongue stale from liquor.

Between the judge and the landscape of lies
where the Supreme Court promotes prostitution,
the world of small ones reels in cruel pain.

The rigged trophy worn over universal jeers,
the cabal of arrogant chiefs swaggers
between cadavers and fire-spitting cavalries.

Between the politician and his image-makers,
between the crusader for oil and his father,
fire consumes fresh leaves; groans in silence

and the minstrel lashes at them whose god is
a murderer in disguise of immaculate white.
Between them, the cemetery of rent hearts!

Oshue

(for leading the anti-tax revolt against the British colonizers in the
Niger Delta)

I

Today the community gathers to remember you,
eighty years after your loud no to the head tax

and asking others not to pay for your God-given head to
a fellow human being however desperate to enrich himself.

If life was so good for the hawk in the sky,
why would it descend so low to kidnap chickens

to fatten itself? England surely needed to grow, but
not on theft. You assembled every village and town

to challenge the district officer's order to pay
for what is surely a human right, one's head.

Walker, the police commissioner, rampaged everywhere;
every adult male fled into hiding and tiptoed in the land—

Walker is out with his force of whips and clubs; beware.
The oyibo cometh, the robber tormentor is here; hide.

What humiliation did men not suffer in the name of collecting
the head-tax for the king who extorts others for England!

When pressed to relieve themselves, should men hold on
to avert being caught outside and thrown straight into jail

for not acceding to robbery the thieves called head tax?
Should men not walk free in their land for fear of force?

Walker is out with his force of whips and clubs; beware.
The oyibo cometh, the robber tormentor is here; hide.

One man stood up, the forefinger in the crowd on the palm,
to cry no to daylight robbery with guns, clubs, and whips.

II

Oshue, you stood out knowing you were exposed to the robber's
weapons; you came out to rally a counter force to the invaders.

You soon gathered a force and appointed commanders—
Otuedor of Gbogidi, Eyube of Agbarho, and other legions.

At Igbudu you were declared His Majesty by the people
who chose you to be king of fighters against foreign tutelage.

Then with all the imperial power of England and their mean spirit,
the DO and his force penned you down for torture and determent.

You suffered jail terms and said whatever the length
would not make you disavow the truth of your fight

because truth does not change nor can it be bent
and still remain the truth; you defended your own.

They buried you to the neck and thought you would recant
but you asked the English torturers to cover your head

so that you would die a free man resisting slavery
and exposing their religion of cruelty and shame;

you would not fear the arms and faces of robbers,
you would not give in to their threats and arrogance.

True scion of warriors, disciple of *Iphri*,* you continued
to turn on the heat to roast your torturers.

III

You asked your people to stop palm oil production,
and they did to stop the sleight of hand called trade;

 your order shut down the factories of those who live
on the sweat of others they con with civilization and lies—

Liverpool, merchant city, became a shadow of itself
because one man far away said no to the armed pillage.

Oshue, you are the first marshal of our army of resistance;
you are the general of hope struggling for truth to triumph.

You did not pay any tax to the foreigners for your head
and generations of Oshues never did—Your Majesty inspires,

and I dedicate this song to you and your commanders
for routing the tax collectors, district officers, and police

despite their torture designs, prayers to a godless lord
and the royal charge to rob the weak to build fortune.

---

* *Iphri:* also spelled "*Ivwri*," Urhobo god of vengeance and restitution.

At Mt. San Angelo, outside the real world

On this early dawn walk, I stop before the real world begins.
Crossing over would be insane, and I retreat to consort
with rabbits, squirrels, bluebirds, blue jays and a pageant
of spring flowers that make the garden of Mt. San Angelo.
I will live outside the real world for as long as I can do so.
Authentic beauty goes uncorrupted by competing fads—
no resident tampers with the divine craftsman's sculpted
image of each; all follow the diurnal rhythm of the mount.
Outside the real world, I live to the full my incredible dreams.
"Within Mt. San Angelo, nobody's been sick," says a composer
who survived a holocaust and travelled golden decades here.
Really there are no doctors, only cooks and servers.
Last night's full moon is entering the trench of daylight.
Peace holds here, with no wars to fund or rigged elections
to contest. Over the mountain girded by ravines, outside
this haven, politicians of all cultures lie for a living.
I won't give up this mountain for another residence
out there recovering from the shock of mass murder.
Here I am not afraid of my tall shadow; no amber alerts.
I will not cross over to the real world this early dawn
for all the dollars and made-up faces out there to chase.
O Aridon, keep me out of the real world for this ecstasy,
the primeval garden of love on this mountain residence.

The cows of Mt. San Angelo

Groomed as royal, the cows of Mt. San Angelo
have the abundant pastures of the mountain
to themselves; evergreen grass all year round.
Plump and healthy, no cows can be bigger
than these multiethnic crop of Virginia cows.
Black, brown and white-faced like a mask,
they mow the grass gracefully; no hostile figures
or irritants to worry about. Young ones
prance to their mothers when I come close,
but there's no fear of poachers in this pasture.

The cows of Mt. San Angelo cannot cover
the entire meadow that's green with abundance.
They know not that outside famine kills a number
and rinderpest and poachers are on the loose.
They are half-covered in lush grass without bother
of ticks—above, birds sing their hearts away
in the paradise they share. There's no Fulani
herdsman lashing at them to take the right course
in the lines they always create in the open space.
They yawn at night from the day's plentiful food.

They have the garden world to themselves—
they know not the harsh struggle or sweat
that each day brings; they are self-assured.
They share the road and their shit bothers none.
If one should be a cow, wouldn't one wish to be
one of the selected cows grazing Mt. San Angelo?
But, after all the pleasures, will the butcher
spare them the fate of other cows envious of them?
The cows of Mt. San Angelo belong to a class
of their own—treated royally for the king's table.

86

For Lady Rose

(in memory of the great Udu singer and performer)

I heard your music and its echoes before I met you—
Godini had so sung your name that it tortured me
until I drove out to buy and play your DVDs.
I knew you were out of this world, voice liberating
and message uplifting the entire body into a spirit.
Once I heard you, there was no dawn without you;
I knew the *otie* fruit had chosen to fall before me.
And then I met you at Otuama's home campaign
after Godini phoned me to abandon whatever on hand
and head to hear Uhaghwa's* favourite perform live.
Singing and dancing, who doubted the gift of the goddess,
that lilting stream in which you performed a divine act?
Still breathing fast, I accosted you with compliments;
still sweating from the frenzy Uhaghwa subjected you to,
I hugged you my sister so proud of your sunny brilliance
and exchanged cards for scions of Aridon to keep company.
And I flew back to listen to you and watch you daily,
waiting to call you and waiting on the muse for words
to further raise you high and sweep you off your feet.
And then the lightning strike: a car crashed into
the motorcycle that carried you; you collapsed into silence.
I had hoped for more meetings, but have been robbed
of the bride of songs, the queen whose kingdom lives.
Lady who traversed my path like a meteor on a dark night,
your songs and gestures will live forever in this song,
the love letter I was writing and practicing to deliver to you.
There will be no death of you, songs and dance alive.

May 3, 2007

---

* Uhaghwa is god of artistic performance and Aridon god of memory among the Urhobo people.

Pride of Bengal

(for Dr. Mahua Mukherjee, Dance Professor)

From the red-glowing star on your forehead
through the costume to your red-ochre feet,
West Bengal bleeds with the shame of injustice.

Once the music entered your veins, you sprang
to the floor, your feet no longer just yours
possessed by the gods of dance in your body.

So majestic the dance steps, moving spirit,
 you so supple and taut, the proud incarnation
of all your people's virtues in one frame.

When it came to the adivasi dance, the throbbing
pain passed to me in the absorbed audience;
the dance of the hermaphrodite an abstract art.

At the flourish of drums, your body opened out,
a lotus that brought out light to outstretched necks.
My adivasi sister, you are *uwara*,* the conscience

that bleeds profusely before a silent adoring world.
After the dance you went down on your knees
to kiss the director's feet for a prize too small for you.

Of your people, their arts hidden to avert praise
from the pompous caste of nitwits and burghers.
You descend from a line of artists, a true *owena*.+

---

* *uwara*: in Urhobo folklore, female tree symbolic of feminine beauty and power.
+ *owena*: master-artist in Urhobo/Pan-Edo areas of Nigeria.

I accosted you for a chat and photo to keep for this day
and you told me of your love of Africa and Africans.
I love you too and we must fight to push out the incubus.

How long is a Brahmin's day more than your own day?
Is there another moon brighter than yours in all of India?
Only one earth holds all; none is master of our joint earth.

Let the robed lords of arrogance and injustice die of shame,
let the upholders of the pillars of oppression collapse;
let West Bengal live with glory. Let the entire world

hold you for your worth, the jewel of Indian soil
after centuries of struggle to raise your head. Let
the sun shine, the blood flow on human flowers.

The gem cannot be the dirt, it's not true.
The goddess cannot be the worshiper, it's not fair.
The master cannot be the slave; no more.

You are the beauty the world seeks to live in happiness,
you are the pride of Bengal despite the tin gods;
Madonna of every imaginable dance step on earth.
.
And wherever you are, doctor of songs and dance,
I crown you queen of divas, my *owena*, with words.
Of course, I do not only touch but embrace you.

Yola's fish

"Eat the fish caught from the Benue at Yola
and you'll return to the city to settle or visit,"
says Ola at the fish treat of the July evening.
One, he warned, who ate the fish, continued
to postpone leaving Yola for another day
that turned into weeks, months, and years,
and has lived another decade after the dish.
I had at every visit gone to my favourite joint
to have fish and Gordon's Spark and returned.
This circular path of the fish I have embraced
and look forward to visiting Yola without end,
always back to the dish that begs for another round,
a spell cast by mysterious love that can't be resisted.

Sukur

(a world heritage place near Madagali in Nigeria's Adamawa State)

These wonders lie protected by distance
now opened for public viewing.

Sukur has lived till today
 because buried in stone;

the chief's voice is heard
because silent by custom.

I come to Sukur by way
of impassable roads,

the novelty an ancient secret
whose craft is dispersed in stone

piled upon stone, a few openings
to enter and marvel at the closure

of a tale that runs into eons of depth
but needs no excavation to tell whole.

After reading Yehuda Amichai

Time does not reside inside the clock or watch
whatever the brand and however precise it works.

A house has walls and doors to keep one in or out,
but refuge or security opens or closes its own space.

Let the clock or watch tell whatever time it wishes,
late or fast in a grand design beyond its body;

there, never captured in the house built for it,
time rolls on inexorably, a flood down a cliff

into an ocean that gives land the chance
to boast of its capacity to be the human habitat.

I often think of the voice inside the gramophone,
the image in the mirror, the shadow and not the body.

However precise or expensive the brand of clock or watch,
time resides elsewhere, far from the gold or silver-tinted face.

For the sake of love

What judgment love makes!
What judgment love makes!

He slaughtered a cow for her;
she fell for who offered a chicken.

What a mystery love is!
What a mystery love is!

She spiced and fried mudfish for him;
he fell for who boiled bony tilapia.

What a foolish thing love is!
What a foolish thing love is!

She asked him to assist with a light load;
he declined it for another's crushing bundle.

What a riddle love can be!
What a riddle love can be!

He married who captured him
rather than whom he captured.

What a changing thing love is!
What a changing thing love is!

He accepted her white for black,
she took his full cup as only half.

What a diverse experience love is!
What a diverse experience love is!

The young lick fresh wounds,
the old ignore scars and go on.

What a secret love is!
What a secret love is!

When it hurts you want to flee,
when it heals you seek it with life.

What a fool I have been!
What a philosopher I can be!

For the Black Pharaohs

They broke your nose to foreclose
your returning to claim lordship of the Two Lands;
they thought they tore up your roots
out of Egypt that was your dominion,
but you still live astride the Two Lands
and remain the buttress of the tall tree.
Piye* kept invaders far away from his neighbours
and won't wish a lion to devour his enemy.
Tuharqua ruled for over two decades and withdrew.
And Queen Tiye exercised sovereignty over the land.
On the stelae your promises remain.
The pyramids you built still stare at God above.
To you, black Pharaohs, there's surely life
after death, and you prosper there and here.

---

* Piye, Tuharqua, and Queen Tiye were black pharaohs.

Benin

The moats filled with sand and weeds;
three broken rings of dynastic fortifications.

The leopard lives a prized bronze artwork,
the mirror of a pouncing past when proud.

Don't ask me why the land's devastated,
the people distraught by a swarm of locusts.

A rogue cock daily crows in dawn
after the sun's bloodied by gunfire,

but out of the red soil a new crop sprouts
cornucopia that beats out corrupt power.

New Year in New Delhi, 2008

The refurbished double-decker monster had vomited out a crowd.
The countdown began at the tail of the immigration snake, one of many.
Every eye glued to the television, all other activities froze.
At the flash of 2008 we burst into Happy New Year, a chorus
and strangers shook hands for good wishes of a brand-new year.
Outside the luggage area, by the customs officers, Indians distributed
a local cake, they said, meant a new year of happy prospects. Nobody
turned down this gift that wraps an entire year with happiness.

Outside the pre-paid taxi section, CHOTRO[*] staff waited behind
the welcoming rails. Davis, Baxal, and Sef shook hands: "You're
welcome."
Cecile, German lady, had arrived earlier from Paris. Into a minivan
we poured for the drive to guest houses scattered all over town.
Cecile in flowing English sang *Cecilia, don't break my heart*—
she's been married for sixteen years. We talked African literature,
the novel trends of globalization, gender and the hermaphrodite of
    sexuality.
I took my colleagues back to Ekwensi's *Jaguar Nana*; nothing new.

As we entered the old city, a haze of dust; I hadn't escaped the harmattan.
How much of a spacious landscape milling with millions could we see
this night in which Delhi sleepwalked excitedly, driving carefree
heavy trucks, cars, and an armada of marutis[+] abreast as if in one motion?
Along eye-stretching avenues, the night sped on and on into the horizon
until at *The Times of India* we stopped for direction to the Science
Academy.
Everyone got lost in the belly of the beast, a transparent maze of
crossings.
Off we took in another direction into the night seeking the city centre.

---

[*] CHOTRO: India-based organization for the protection of the earth and indigenous peoples led by
    Ganesh Devy.
[+] *maruti*: Indian three-wheel van used as a taxi.

In a language of early dawn, strange and smooth the night sped on
until the Indian Science Academy—the stop for me to sign in at 2:03 a.m.
Knocking at the door for a roommate, Tonukari opened with joy.
"Prof, just a minute," after hearing Urhobo amidst Hindi mutterings.
After courtesies, sharing space, and introduction to the room,
I changed into sleeping clothes and without much ado dived into bed.
I would wake before New Year began in either Charlotte or Warri.
That's New Year's Eve in Delhi, a fascinating first as never before.

For Mahatma Gandhi

The assassin's bullet could not wipe out
your last steps to the prayer house
nor the interminable group listening to your words there.

And so barefoot, I walked the steps and sat cross-legged
and listened in over fourteen languages to your message
of transforming the scoundrel world without spilling blood.

I concur with your message. You walked barefoot
in sack cloth over broken bottles on your way
to reach untouchables across the vast land of India,

but you were not just Indian or even South African
but a prophet of the human spirit, the entire world
sent by sky and earth to save those trodden underfoot.

I gave my words: *Mahatma Gandhi, owho uyota ve
ufuoma ohore vwo ke iwho akpo eje. Ufuoma dia ke we!*[*]
Countless languages of the world speak your truth.

Today I bow to you for the peaceful sacrifice of your life.
Neither gun nor bomb can obliterate your steps or message
that I follow here, footmarks etched into everlasting memory.

Now the elites may not know where your ashes rest,
but hundreds of thousands of poor ones from India and Asia
continue to stream here because you stood for them

---

[*] Urhobo for "Mahatma Gandhi, man of truth / and peace who fought for all humans. Peace be onto you!"

in their remote and rugged terrains scarred by hurting flesh that groans from the weight of obscene overlords without qualms strutting streets and corridors of power.

To be named Victor

(for Victor Umukoro)

To be named Victor and not vanquish the demons after him,
to be a warrior whose amulets failed before spells of vagrancy,
to lose the way to his destination and the direction back home

how do I mourn a friend who set out without returning?
Somewhere he is alive but dead; somewhere dead but alive—
I run into him now and then, a stranger I can't recognize;

neither a ghost to run from nor someone to embrace.
He mounted a motor bike and rode into the blinding sun;
no compass to thread together his footmarks and clothes.

The ageing domestic cat seeks refuge in the vast forest,
the python forsakes the travails of the forest for deep waters—
it is where the call comes from that the soul leads one.

He must be living in the forest, river, soil, or somewhere;
he lives in a space he rode to and embraced, subsumed—
his future like a torchlight whose batteries stopped working.

Maybe he lived out his entire life and rode into thin air
without saying "I won't come back" to friends and neighbours;
maybe in other lands he found peace and decided to expire.

Named Victor from birth, he evaporated on a simple journey—
he couldn't clutch life to his chest for as long as he wished!
Where he eventually arrived would be everybody's guess.

He did not return from his daylight ride into clouds of dust;
his hope did not bring him back on another motor bike.
I think of Victor neither dead nor alive, just somewhere.

The humility of the wise

Ten years ago the bull was just a calf,
now his brows scare off sheep from the field

last year the reed survived because of no torrents,
this year it dances confidently in the face of hurricanes

three months ago the crocodile hatched one of its eggs,
today another crocodile exercises dominion over the waters

only several weeks ago the moon was a slice of no consequence,
tonight it has waxed full to glisten in a brilliant gesture.

When an initiate the fear of the angry god was paramount,
now the angry priest and the god speak in one voice.

Great wishes

The tortoise wishes it possessed a cheetah's leap
to flash through fields rifled with peril,

the cheetah wishes it had a castle like the tortoise's
to perpetually guard against marauders;

the chameleon wishes its costume didn't change colours
but flaunted an identity no one took for granted;

the black anthill wishes it didn't live a sedentary life
and be the laughingstock of all passersby.

The minstrel accepts his fate of songs
that carries tears and laughter in one voice.

III

FLOW & OTHER POEMS

For Marho

also in her special place

Don't tell the weeping eye that it can't see
the catastrophe that the bridge holds at bay.

Wetin Man Go Do?

Wetin man go do?
The poet asks his muse.

The goat gets so pressed,
it defecates as it moves.

Wetin man go do?
It asks in apology.

The tortoise wipes out
everybody's only food.

Wetin man go do?
It asks in self-defence.

Ogun litters the wide road
with scrap metal and bones.

Wetin man go do?
He asks fellow gods.

The general executes
his rivals in a coup.

Wetin man go do?
He asks the army hierarchy.

The politician rigs
his way into power.

Wetin man go do?
He asks party loyalists.

The lover jilts his partner
to embrace a fresh face.

Wetin man go do?
He asks the flirting heart.

The pastor threatens
the congregation with hell fire.

Wetin man go do?
He asks jealous Jehovah.

The coffin-seller starts the day
with prayers for brisk business.

Wetin man go do?
He asks the god of fortune.

The udje singer wishes misfortune
to strike rivals for songs of ridicule.

Wetin man go do?
He asks his mentor-god.

The poet proclaims
a festival of songs.

Wetin man go do?
He asks his muse.

I No Go Sidon Look[*]

I no go sidon look
like African Union soja for Darfur

I no go sidon look
make Shell dey piss and shit for our water

I no go sidon look
make Pentecostal noise cover *udje* drums

I no go sidon look
make anybody curse Mama wen born me

I no go sidon look
make hawk come catch my neighbour fowl for my yard

I no go sidon look
make thief just dey chop like that

I no go sidon look
make cobra tanda for my door-mouth

I no go sidon look
I go clap for swordfish when kill crocodile

I no go sidon look
I go throw party for black ant wen fall elephant

I no go sidon look
I go dance when hyena die

I no fit sidon look lailai
I go do something-o.

---

[*] *Sidon look* is the Pidgin English for "sit down and look"; that is, remain passive.

Out of Step

"I have stopped reasoning" (Oladele Akogun)

I

They tell me witches have made the cherry fruit tree
their coven where they plot the death of their kinsfolk
who die of diabetes, stroke, heart-attack, and cancer.

These victims of witches did not guard against cholesterol
and had their fill of palm oil, coconut, and larded beef.
They relished their staple of starch, garri, yam, and rock salt.

They argue that not working hard matters not for a nation
and stealing from public coffers impedes no development.
They say rigging elections or not voting is part of democracy.

I hear them say a madman is the best pilot they have had
while a drunkard is the diviner they seek for salvation.
They say one blinded by lust is leading them out of poverty.

My born-again people abandon the ways others emulate
and spit at the graves of parents who spoke to plants;
they burn the arts for which the rest of the world marvels.

"I have stopped reasoning," says my friend, when the populace
of swarming witches, converts, drunks, robbers, and mad ones
say that he's out of step with reality and so not their kinsman.

II

With the goatish behaviour of my country folks,
 heads stuffed with starch in place of brains,
they walk on their heads where others sprint.

Inside a dark hole they daydream daily of standing
in the air on a hill that touches the sun, resplendent.
I have stopped reasoning with a lunatic population.

Living with those who believe they can trick quiet God
by showering him praises and knocking him from behind,
believing the all-knowing blind and so can be deceived.

I have stopped reasoning with adherents of a strange faith;
the same ones who raped Olokun with a smile and believing
their wealth would redouble with the forbidden blood of ritual!

My country men and women swagger with their backs to
where the rest of the world, out of breath, races forward.
I have stopped reasoning with those out of step with life.

III

When babies wore beards, I saw reason in the phenomenon
of the ending and the beginning in a flux of old and young.
Pieces of an old yam grow to fill a barn with fresh produce.

I know not why the ancestors are left with bones of animals
sacrificed to them, while priest and devotees feast on the flesh.
Residents of the other world are too dumb to argue their rights.

My people believe the nation will grow into a super power
as they laze about on imported luxuries, the industry of others.
We seek the technology to transplant the iroko to the desert.

Demons are carousing in churchyards to the alleluias of converts.
My people cannot see the world as a chain which binds them to others.
I have stopped reasoning with those who deny their own humanity.

I Sing Out Of Sickness

(for Ebi, after asking: "What makes you write?")

I am sick from chasing robbers that take me for granted
with whips that don't flog and shouts they shut ears from hearing

sick from the lethargic silence of my kinsfolk who suffer
racking pain that doses of pirated Codeine cannot relieve

sick from seeing folks timorous of their endowment
that would enable them smash their scourge and be safe

sick from the blindness of people from under whom lords tap
their wealth and insult them for the misery that breaks the heart.

I am mad at the harrowing hunger churning at them
and cannot go on watching and doing nothing with the pellets

fired at them without provocation as if to tame their restive stomachs
and children possessed into demons and branded militants; loathed.

I always chase the lords and their livery of dominion
and only singing without stop provides me respite.

And I throw up at the nauseating body that has become
my land, the once primeval beauty splotched and scarred;

I throw up because I am thirsty in the midst of streams
that flow black pus from poisoned veins now varicose,

dying from sunstroke in the rainforest once a divine canopy
now beheaded by poachers out to choke insatiable sawmills.

And sometimes I am lost in the deep night of my wanderings,
the entire neighbourhood a blackout policed by armed robbers;

then in the pandemonium I look for a way out to be sane
and remain human without humiliating my manhood

especially with drunken soldiers and police on the loose
locking down towns and roads to celebrate their delirium.

Always the orphan gets arrested for killing the sacred cow
and no one who knows the real culprit exonerates the poor one.

Paid party thugs hijack the visionary's electoral votes;
pirates offload the gifted nation's fortune at sea.

Male worshipers gang-rape their goddess
in the belief that her bleeding will flower into billions.

Now victors are condemned to victims,
the wails of the wounded intensify;

tomorrow thieves will be monarchs, governors, and presidents
to the praise chants of ghost writers and red caps.

The world must not crash before holding back harassing hands;
we must not leave it to lightning alone to strike down the monster.

I run into an unknown landscape a fugitive seeking peace
in a wilderness that harbours hope for the desperate

whose nightmares would light into a refuge of stars
breaking out of nowhere to transform the demons.

This is the life that releases the enchanting songs
that mob my days and nights in a perpetual siege

and I helpless and dazed beyond words of testimony
that get lost before they arrive at their destined end.

I sing out of sickness from multiple afflictions,
sing from the pain of knowledge without memory.

On Environmental Day

(at Effurun)

Everyone is asked by the state to stay at home
and clean the surroundings; no movement
on the street and highway to keep the ban.
Violators not in high places expect thrashing.
I wish other days would be promulgated:
Truth Day to eliminate the litters of lies
that allow no integrity to sprout in the land;
Honesty Day to curb armed robberies at home
and highways that make a war zone of the state;
Secular Day to silence the cacophonies of alleluias
that drown peace in pastoral ranting for collections;
Human Day to transform the dressed vulgar animals
into feeling human beings of men and women;
Patience Day to rein in the craze for wealth that drives
recklessly over so many others on the way to prosperity;
Law and Order Day to make a country of riotous ones
always follow the line and give way to emergency traffic;
Modesty Day to strip the pompous rogues of their brocades
and expose the splotches the titled ones cover for a living.
Declare Corruption-Free Day and the nation disappears
without politicians, police, army, and *follow-follow* citizens.
So many other days remain to be promulgated, including
Personal Hygiene Day, Forgiveness Day, and above all Peace Day
for without any order we care not for a clean environment.
We care not for ourselves and the neighbours that sustain our lives;
for every day, not the month's last Saturday, is Environmental Day
just as every day in the calendar of life must be Humanity Day.

July 26, 2008

Narratives of Gold

(after visiting a jeweller at Wuse Market, Abuja)

The jewellers at Wuse Market welcome you warmly
to their sheds filled with millions in assortments of gold—
mostly yellow and occasionally white; silver stays away.
They buy, exchange, and sell gold—their scales
and calculators ready for whatever transaction sought.
"Today the price of gold has gone up," one explains,
and I cherish a trader telling the truth that hurts his profit,
a rare commodity in the market of fortune seekers.
One of my colleagues sells a necklace for forty-two thousand
naira, a gain of twenty thousand after wearing it for ten years.
She was satisfied with the bargain she struck in several minutes.
Another colleague wants to buy high-quality gold
to treat herself after reimbursement of a long overdue payment.
Of GL, the Hausa jeweller says: "It's only coated with gold
but not pure." "What of Italian gold?" the prospective buyer asks.
"That's good but many others are better," he says like a sage.
He goes on to tell how Saudi is better than Italian,
Dubai superior to Saudi, and Indian the highest priced.
He talks of carats that mean much to the price placed on gold;
for him 18 carats the standard in his gold-lavished shop.
After toying with white gold, my celebrating colleague
settles for a Dubai set of earrings and necklace to dazzle.
She paid a ponderous sum, smiling to out-shine the gold.
As soon as she pays, at about six, the jeweller shuts his shed,
and I leave with a fresh sense of gold, not the glittering metal
but a complex possession with so many long narratives.

July 22, 2008

Wafi,* My Incontestable Love

I

Wafi is saturated with prayers, soaked in tears:

pain paints the streets with harsh colours;
a nightmarish sun and a depressed moon.

The contested city littered with aborted dreams,
the sick seek no cure from medication but chants;

the poor doomed in abysmal debts and denials,
every day held hostage to impossible demands.

Warri is soaked in tears, saturated with prayers.

II

In Warri the outsider stands out.
"*Yawa* don gas," the locals say.
"I beg your pardon!" the stranger exclaims.

"Which kind *kpele* you be
say you no dey hear man?"
the perplexed locals ask;

to them the world revolves round the hood;
the oil city holds the entire world to ransom.
"What are you saying?" the outsider asks.

"Okpe-e! Those your ears na horse ears?
I see! Not everyone wen dey pick teeth
eat better meat. You dey Wafi; Wafi no dey you!"

---

* Local slang for "Warri". Thought to originate from the acronym of the defunct Warri Football Association ,WAFA. Used to be "Wafa City", now simply "Wafi".

Ricochets of bullets perforate dusk into dawn.
"That na gunshot or knockout?" the locals ask,
as the outsider takes to his heels for dear life.

III

Shuo-o! Which kind gbreghe be this?
Wafi man no dey carry last-o.
No be me go fail my people.

Nobody go see my brake light
before I reach where I dey go.
Wafi man no dey carry last.

Where you see fowl beat eagle for flight?
Who born them say they go run pass spirit.
I be spirit—nobody fit pass me for road.

For everywhere Wafi man no dey fail-o.
Wafi man no dey carry last.
I be correct Wafi man. I no go carry last.

IV

The Warri man leaves town for Abuja or London
and his brain shrinks—unless you get close
to a sleeping chicken, you won't know it snores!

He goes against traffic, not knowing the rules he obeys
are jungle customs the rest of the world has shunned.
"No be so they dey do-am?" he asks, the king of fools.

"E-he," he continues, disarmed after stubborn resistance.
In Warri everybody fights over nothing, at best over trifles,
and outside the rascal shouts where there should be silence.

Then it's the new locals' turn to laugh at the *oburhobo*
newly come to real town. Warri is a deep hole

whose residents glamorize threadbare existence.
The Warri migrant has no starch to wack;
no *oghwo* to relish. He soon falls in love with
others and forgets the royal dish of commoners.

V

The Warri homeboy returns from abroad
and the chastened braggart talks low
to the consternation of his home-trapped fellows.

He spews out new vocabs: "How far?" he asks,
and doesn't wait to be asked fresh questions.
He knows not the new idioms and songs,

and becomes the butt of the street's jibes—
new idioms enter the lingo at an alarming rate. Now
they delete their enemies and then download them.

And to everybody's delight men insert
their SIM cards night and day; hence
the town now overflows with babies!

VI

City, eternally stuck in a compressor,
you are the world shrunk to a mere dot.
What makes you so different from others?

To be born in Warri and roam its streets
is to be a Wafi man, a king of fools
too self-absorbed to see others as human.

Swegbe![*] City of a cursing crowd where
parents swear obscenities at their children
and young folks damn their elders, learn.

---

[*] Slow, dim-witted person!

No one is king over one's self but over others
who deny dominion and hurl curses at the fool
whose blindness deceives him of nowhere else

but where he stands—a playground that's
nothing better than the closed backyard of others.
Warri, learn. Your language is a difficult one.

City in which visitors need interpreters,
you are smart enough to make others laugh
at themselves in public and cry alone in bed;

but neither hospitable nor hostile, what a host!
City of blues with folks so full of themselves,
Warri, you remain my incontestable love.

Contribution to the National Debate

1

In the daydream of the madman
he saves the commonwealth from a nightmare

brandishing toy guns at invading armies
and singing their anthem before a column of ants

when indeed he trashes the national flag
and mauls the eagle that stretches vision.

In his grand delusion the priest believes
he is the last prophet of his lost people;

he swaggers with a combustible walking stick
and sees not where the road plunges into a chasm

even as he offends the god of fortune
whose anger he daily draws upon the land.

2

One man's farm cannot fill the dinner tables of
the entire nation even if the farmer were President,

one man's charities however far stretched
cannot cover the horizons of the large state;

one man out of a hundred and fifty million
should not tie his people to the tail of his tiger.

Thunder strikes the iroko, king of all trees,
and the rainforest still wears its evergreen;

Olotu,* invincible in his young days, falls
and the army marches on to fresh battles.

One farmer however large his farm should not
feed compatriots with the flatulence of greed;

everybody deserves a farm to savour self-raised crops.
One should not take for granted the lies of the elder

who wants the young to clap for his farts.
There's more to a republic than an old head,

a coconut that can fall overnight without a storm.
One man's short-sighted measure isn't the nation's vision.

3

Three times will be too long to allow
the nude emperor to fool the populace
with his patented brand of brocade;

three terms of a monstrous birth
will wreck the mother beyond recognition
and lose all pride and beauty.

Three sessions of the obscene dance
will make crow and king bury the state in tears
and Abuja will forever remain a laughingstock;

three robberies of ballot boxes in a decade
impoverish the nation beyond recovery
and the general will bleed democracy to death.

Three bland songs from the same crow
will send the sad country's folks to sleep
and not wake until another night.

---

* Olotu: Urhobo word for chief warrior.

119

Testimony to the Nation's Wealth

Unending expanse of rain-flushed savannah
with lost settlements of sorely clad folks
in thatched and rusted tin homes discovered and
counted in preordained censuses and elections.
Lonesome roads of peeled or cracked tarmac
and potholes inviting a cortege of accidents
at every corner and intersection of fading paths.
With representatives carousing in faraway Abuja,
the land flaunts a tattered flag of hopeless faces—
*white and green** make no sense of dire sovereignty.
When there's a conflagration of the assembly,
they flee to the forgotten land of their ancestors
where the silenced folks half-gone in hunger
summon hidden spirits into their anaemic bodies,
burst into praise chants and gyrate to drums
for their heroes, hyenas, visiting them for once.
I sing blues of the national wealth after driving
with headaches from Bauchi through Gombe
to Yola, state capitals whose total allocations
exceed entire incomes of many robust nations.

---

* *white and green*: Nigeria's national flag.

120

On Poverty Day, 2008

I see tears beneath brows made-up
to pass the day's inescapable trials;

I watch bravado acts of cowards
already broken down by denials.

I no longer call harsh names
in the famished world of

lazybones, prostitutes, and beggars
who have nothing else to live on

as deflated princes and princesses
pant in agony, their sole refuge.

Now they proliferate the land:
prostitute queens and beggar kings,

kwashiorkor princes and princesses
posthumously inheriting the earth

of parents squeezed out of their lineage
pawned out their pride and property

for the supply of biscuits and kola nuts
that made them loyal to vultures.

The citizenship of whores hurts the heart,
the notion of nobility dead and buried;

the paraphernalia in tatters, snatched
by falcons after the flesh to sate hunger.

More than every other one is down,
as much short of pride as of cash.

*   *   *

Dispense with representatives and pastors
of walking barebones

strike dumb chanters of prayers
preying on frail flesh

cut down elders leading backwards
to the Stone Age that breaks backbones

delete the anthem of *hammer**
from the lips of desperadoes

lockjaw to preachers of prosperity
to folks without faith in humanity

bury the alleluias of the throng
seeking salvation in corrupted commandments

behead those at the top of the rotten state
amputate the masses sustaining the vulgarity

for there has to be massive deaths
to conceive the *beautyful* ones.+

---

* *hammer:* has to do with opportunism. Derived from a song in which the singer talks about seizing any opportunity to be rich and that involves stealing and corruption

+ *beautyful* ones: as of Ayi Kwei Armah's novel, *The Beautyful Ones Are Not Yet Born.*

Elegy for Nostalgia

How will the ancestral population replenish
itself with the present crop of living folks

still fresh on the stalk falling off without storm;
brushfires ambushing brown and green leaves?

Where will the league of heroes come from
with the takeover of the nation by thieves?

Who will transform into gods to be worshiped
with no respect for followers beneath or behind;

with leaders soiling themselves with scandals,
selling their allegiance to their people's robbers;

seizing from the blind light to recover their rights,
denying the crippled space to exercise humanity?

I am struck by the dearth of goodwill in the neighbourhood,
the abundance of *bad belle* despite alleluias and salaaming;

I raise the cry to build dykes against the rivers of tears,
seek silence from the cacophony of the riotous music.

If history were to die from our hands or in our keep,
what life would be there to live without chroniclers?

If the muse, angry from much needless provocation,
struck dumb the minstrel, what new songs would heal

the gaping wounds that torment folks night and day
or move the tired world higher to a cheerful sphere?

Wish I could engrave more faces on coins or notes, but
it is a tall order to find them to fill the vacancies ahead.

I seek resuscitation of the dying breed of the earth
to sing of ancestors, heroes, gods, and chroniclers.

The Tortoise Trainer

(after seeing Osman Handi Bey's "The Tortoise Trainer" at the
Islamic Arts Museum Malaysia)

I have become a tortoise trainer.
I have a pool of hot water nearby
to deter from slipping underwater
to escape the vengeance of victims.
I practice my profession in a clearing;
here, neither mahoganies nor irokos
with their massive multiple roots
to hold to when I pull back the villain
to appear in court and face the verdict.
Petulant tar beauties stand guard—
if the thief steals before their blind
watch and still slaps to spite them,
it will get stuck till arrested at dawn
and marched across town carrying
its loot. No trillions in the treasury
for the sly one to squander at home
and stash away in complicit banks;
no feathers to borrow to a heavenly
banquet and be the All-of-You
at the famished people's expense.
I won't take my eyes off the trainee
when flavoured beans sit on the fire—
overriding avarice will stir flames
to scald its already scarred head;
the ogre already frightens enough.
I've acquired equipment for the task
of training tortoise after tortoise
because my community is a flock
of hunchbacks, porters of castles,
wearing a patchwork armour of steel
cunning to the bone and so scary.

I am the tortoise trainer of a pack
of one hundred and forty million;
no human to take at face value.

Flow

We flow into each
other as a rule of life:

streams into river,
rivers into ocean

roads into town,
people into workplace

time into spaces,
place into history

things into beings,
persons into things

night into day,
dark into light

wetness into drought,
oases into dunes

evergreens into rust,
harvest into planting

company into solitude,
single into couple

chaos into calm,
ruins into magnificence

spirit into body,
body into soil.

I am in a circle
binding me with others,

replenishes youth
with experience;

death with life,
fear with courage;

the two parts of one.
I accept to be human

to live one life
flowing into others

I do not even know
but of the same earth

we share as partners
in the living present

as one flow aware
of ever flowing.

The Ethiope at Abraka, 2008

For the good luck of staying north of the Delta,
for the fate of no oil wells expected in the area

the Ethiope saunters gracefully towards the Atlantic
with the same agility of youth as of timeless age,

the same clarity the water displays from source
through serene forests to the ocean's open arms

that forty years ago as a student I knew at Obinomba
and on midterm break swam the eyes red at Abraka.

The mirroring white sand still dazzles,
the virginal smell of centuries persists

as the deceptive depth of the river
that sheets of white sand still cover.

As I stroll along the riverside, at the beach
that Gordon's Hotel created for recreation,

I collect white stones of diverse shapes
dredged deep from the river's bosom;

I take away in a bottle wet sand pumped
through metal pipes to widen the beach

that nobody has touched before me
and remains pure from inattention.

Truly, there are exceptions to the poaching
oil lords' reach and greed in the land;

truly, there are limits to the business
of concession-selling by the state.

And the exceptions gladden the heart
for so long tormented by despoliation.

The River Niger at Lokoja

No more the majesty that blew the heart away—
opulent sheet billowing in the wind every season;

the beauty that tested the temerity of foreigners
and their concession now half gone from afflictions.

Strings of puddles litter the valley with muddy water;
new islets break the once glistening flow seaward—

neither at the sunrise start from the mountain, the supple
bend at Djenne a sleek course that assembled wise ones

nor at the delta, no longer a web of wetland creeks
but clogged arteries that threaten the river's life.

Today fishers no longer throw their nets, set hooks
nor women wade through with scooping baskets;

children no longer dodge house chores to swim, nor
travellers ply the waterways infested with hyacinths.

The beauty has slipped from the majesty of ages
to a rickety figure unable to turn bends with speed

and moves a drained runner out of breath dragging
feet and entire body through inhospitable terrains.

Dams have damned the fate of one divined for majesty;
despite frog-croaking downpours the body dehydrated

and now lives without its proverbial gusto of flow;
immobile from dastardly blows suffered for centuries

in the name of human needs and development projects
that generate hunger and cut off the primeval lifeline.

No more the majesty that takes the breath away,
the beauty suffering so many human afflictions.

At Myrtle Beach

I

Fire-bristling ball of orange
atop the wave-lashing beach

glittering mirror of gold
petals kiss my forehead

as breeze after breeze
salutes the new dawn.

Horizons stretch eyes
into infinite waters

whose bottom warrior waves
protect from massive poaching.

The beach is a smiling nation
of citizens enjoying a holiday

wishing to live that way forever
but must return after the sun sinks

into dreams that are tasks that
hands must carry out with zeal.

II

I know my footmarks will vanish
with the wave-long assault on land

long before the crowds arrive
with cameras that miss the beauty

long before the sharks come
ashore to test their bloody skills

long after Mami Wata retreats
into her palace to live without guards

and lovers hold hands strolling, not
knowing the goddess already blessed

one who stares across the Atlantic
at another singing the water song

that both know bridges the divide
and brings them together

to celebrate one long dream,
the music of their heartbeat.

III

I can never say goodbye to the sea
that keeps my peace alive and going

in the infinite wealth of the vast basin
that nobody can exhaust with lust.

I can never leave the water-maid alone
if my love for the best must persist.

I can only wish for a return
to invoke from the deeps my love

always fresh and resplendent
after the absence we must suffer

to rededicate our bodies and minds
to the permanence of water in us.

I leave the beach at this hour
when adulators mob the sand

unaware of the hallowed ground
the divine one sanctified with waves.

I must leave the beach now as
beer cans and cigarettes litter the sand

and bodies without minds and souls
stretch naked to tan pale skins.

I can never leave the waters;
I carry Mami Wata always in my heart

that beats with the relentless spirit:
one whose love is the greatest wealth.

The Malay Testament

1. *At the KLCC Twin Towers*

I choose to spend my day high up
beyond the pale of plebeian eyes.

I can now boast of climbing the tallest
building on the planet of rival shafts.

At this supernatural height, will my hands
pluck alien fruits from the sun or moon?

How many sky gods can I rival
in this human elevation of steel?

Can I now converse with the Almighty
whose throne sits on my naughty head?

Can I commune with residents of galaxies
the pompous earth refuses to acknowledge?

I laugh at the human craft of gestures
belittling gods as if smaller than humans.

2. *Open House*

One day in the year the legislator must
throw his house open to his people

to see him close, shout things at his ears so that
he knows what to take back to the assembly.

One day the representative hosts his community,
reiterates the duty for which he lives in the capital;

always talks on their behalf, meets on their behalf
and has to appropriate their voice to be worthy

of their sacred mission from home to the gathering
of the nation that is now their business to regulate.

The link between delegate and people must not be
broken; one must continue to be part of others:

the leader must host those he represents in Putra Jaya;
the people must come to see how their emissary lives

and draw their own conclusions from what they see
to know how to vote when the next election comes.

The Ancient Greeks would squirm at this practice
but the Malays and others arrived at this before them:

humanity definitely predates democracy
and democracy thrives only on humanity.

3. *Watching*

It's Ramadan and I enter a Malay restaurant
on Armand Street at six-thirty. I can barely
get a place—a crowd of couples and singles
already seated and waiting to break their fast,
waiting for the cry to confirm sunset in the East.
Intriguing to me, luscious plates already set:
dates, bananas, watermelon, and all fruit colours.
Some already ordered tea that will surely cool
before the imam's cry reverberates across town.
A man and his buddy have on their table
lamb chops blackened with a myriad of spices;
others alone or in groups with plates spilling
over with mouth-watering dishes for the rich.
They stare at the steaming dishes, and now
and then look at their watches they must be

blaming for being too sluggish before 7:14
or rather the sun for punishing them with light.
I inhale the delectable aromas, wondering what
drama I am watching at the approach of dusk.
I order for basic noodles with chicken, a light
plate among the crowd—after all, I last filled up
at a Chinese restaurant whose buffet made me a fool;
unlike my folks here who have been dry since dawn.
I take my time to see the end of the play. As I
swallow my last bite and gulp water with lemon,
the piercing cry comes at long last, and behold
the stampede I cannot tell without blaspheming
against a practice I respect for cleansing humanity.

4. By Custom

By custom and command one week in the year
the Malays must leave the city for the natal home

but often they look for every chance to be back
to the family roots that sustain them everywhere.

One week in a year so that you don't ever forget
however long the road home to your source of life.

Memory should never fade to forget the way home,
the roots must be cherished for the growth upwards;

the link in the chain must never be allowed to break
from the rust to the door keys that long absence causes.

By custom we must continue to be part of the family,
as no one comes to life through an unknown gate.

We shouldn't forget the beginning of life wherever
we may find ourselves in the course of our journeys;

hence the Malays must leave the city for the natal home
by custom and command one week every year of their lives.

5. *Among Schoolchildren*

My hostess sits with the driver in front
of the College's Toyota four-wheeler;
I lounge behind in the owner's corner

heading for a private school to meet
children of a school taught in English
and adopted by my host department.

We drive round and round the quarter
without arriving at our destination
meant to be a quarter hour's drive—

neither the elite driver nor my colleague
who had been there before knew the place;
the appointed hour ticked away in no time.

A phone call and my colleague passes
the phone to the driver. We change direction
to the supposed right location of the school,

but soon discover achieving nothing
until a female guard in a bike comes
to lead the way to the school by the corner.

True to Oriental patience, our hosts
are all smiles to meet us at the gate;
the children seated on mats, clean.

Telling African folktales to Malaysian children
round an imagined fireplace at night,
I mimic the tortoise's tricks to applause.

Then with me they sing African songs
with a smoother voice than I expect.
Children's laughter follows; a clear bell.

In the unscripted question and answer part,
boys and girls come to life; true children.
"Do you miss home?" Of course I do.

"Why were you raised by your Grandma?"
And I tell the "Avwerhoke born girl" tale,
a trickster father among hyena relatives.

By the end of the second fleeting hour,
they have flown to the sky for a banquet
with borrowed feathers; I, All-of-You.

They now know why man and woman
quarrel but can't do without each other;
the first pregnancy, and why the sky is high.

They tell me "Thank you!" in Malay.
I tell them "Wa do-o!" which I translate
into English; reciprocal gestures of the day.

On a day I had felt anxious over what to do,
the lateness did not cool the hospitality.
I have learned more than the schoolchildren.

6. Guest at a Chinese Festival

It's the fifteenth day of the eight lunar month
and the entire sky is ablaze with a full moon;

the most brilliant moonshine yearlong, I'm told.
That's when the Chinese hold the Lantern Festival,

also called the Moon Cake Festival or Mid-Summer
Autumn Festival. Wherever they are worldwide

they come out as Chinese to celebrate the rare clarity.
The performers wear costumes of red and yellow—

red for vitality that possesses everyone into a lion
and yellow of fruits like oranges and gold for wealth.

An assortment of foods assault the palate—
octopus, mushrooms, fungus, duck, and others.

To warm up the night a band of young boys
take the stage in front of eating and drinking tables.

Then comes the Lion's Dance everybody waits for,
after the big-headed god of good luck leads the way.

Loud sharp music by a breathless ensemble scares off
evil spirits that lurk around to be safe for the dance.

Then huge lions—two silver and one golden—spring
into the arena and begin their patented dance.

With royal strides they prance, shoot up and forward,
shake their heads and tails without effort to the music.

A masked figure fans the dancers and places drinks down
to replenish the energy and cool their burning bodies

after the lions lay down after so much possessed dance—
they drink Carlsberg and I wonder how come lions love beer.

For a whole hour such choreographed animal dance
that dazed me the only foreigner in the Chinese circle.

At the end the costumes lift off and behold two boys—
head and tail of each lion—that draw ear-splitting applause.

The children rush in to solve puzzles on papers
they have studied and hanging over the clan hall.

The finale: lighting of the lanterns—setting candles
in a collapsible paper lantern to hang on tree branches

or carried about slung on a stick by excited kids.
This the only day Chinese children play with fire;

seated outside lighting and blowing out candles
on a day like no other in their rich calendar of fun.

At the end of the show I tell my hosts "Xie xie!"
thanking them for this festival that reminds me

of Okpara's Elephant Festival last seen fifty years ago,
wondering why humans everywhere take on animal habits.

7. *Putra Jaya*

Of memories, there are no
dark holes in your contour.
Glass skin of Orient blaze,
your moisturized breath tempers
the sun's power with mercy.
You choose to wear green
rather than damask or jacquard.
Of remembrance, you stand
self-assured of your task of
today's sweat, tomorrow's miracle.
You conquered nightmares
not with invocations or chants
but with an unblinking gaze
at the rising sun absorbing
light to dissolve darkness.
It's no longer dream that's
your fort; you already stand
on a hill that encompasses
all directions of possibilities.
I remember your special face
crafted to raise praise songs;

and there's your patented smile
with that tropical warmth
and abandon of hospitality.
Putra Jaya, it's not postcards
of curved bridges, crafted
buildings, and waterfronts
nor the ride and walk on
the Malay Appian Way
that bring me back to you
from another world;
it's the graceful poise
that sets you ready
to conquer coming centuries
with faith in your strides.

Traveller

In Kuala Lumpur
carry an umbrella

in Syracuse
wear snow boots

in the Sahara
tie a face swath

in Burutu
row a boat

in space
keep a lifejacket

on earth
you are a traveller.

At the Akosombo Dam

"It's no more a river but a lake,"
the engineer guide says as he points
to the long expanse of water; "It's now
the Volta Lake, the largest of its kind."
They blasted the rocky mountain nearby
to block the great river; they decapitated it
not with concrete but piles of broken rock
to forever forestall seepage at any level.
The river's majestic flow arrested by force,
the fish population imprisoned to produce
and die without ever entering the Atlantic.
Of course, the lauded project boosted
electricity and development of the nation.
Nobody considers the plight of villagers
ejected, relocated outside ancestral lands.
None among the developers ever thinks
of the beauty of the current cut off its course,
nor of the postcard mountains with waterfalls,
the millennial plants and millions of small lives
not reckoned with in planning and executing
schemes making life abundant for humans.
By the dam the Volta Hotel for tourists;
often opulent foreigners hiding behind
scarred bodies throwing monies at bottles
and waiters for vacations making no meaning
to the annihilation done to leap forward.
And I had earlier sung praises of Ghana
for uninterrupted light, unlike Nigeria
plagued by constant fits in darkness—
how right is wrong and wrong very right!
In the nightmare of masses sits the paradise
of the few powerful wielding their hammer.
Also bulldozers, caterpillars, and dredgers!
There's no more the Volta River but a lake.

You Don't Have to Be

You don't have to be Jewish
to shiver at the nightmare of Auschwitz

you don't have to be black
to feel the agony and shame of slavery

you don't have to be native
to be hurt by the arrogance of discovery

you don't have to be foreign
to know what discrimination means

you don't have to be minority
to understand the dominion of big numbers

you don't have to be homeless
to go through the vagaries of life

you don't have to be rich
to fear the uncertainty of tomorrow

you don't have to be crippled
to suffer the pain of the handicapped

you don't have to be a star
to stare at the volatility of the weather

you just have to be human
to know the plight of others.

Expecting My Bride

Since everybody knew I was expecting a bride,
many prepared to take advantage of my desperation;
they knew who expected a loved one would do anything

to have her come in no time and be swathed in one spread.
They knew my heart would skip a beat with whomever
was called by the name I chanted in my wakeful dream.

A taller lady with the waist of an esoteric wasp entered,
escorted by stars that shone their hearts away expecting
nobody would not be struck by the knockout brilliance,

but I knew she was not the one I waited for these years;
she was not the figure whose face was a mirror
I looked into to see the earth and sky that held me.

The world knew how fast my heart beat as I waited.
I had done this waiting for as long as they knew me
and couldn't expect me not jumping at the opportunity

of one heralded by a flotilla of butterflies of another world;
they expected me to catch the shadow before the body arrived,
since the contours of dawn and dusk overshadow longing.

So another one came, carrying the charm of a gazelle
grazing with abandon the abundance of the savannah
that multiplied with every season of rain and growth.

They knew not I needed not every charm, even that
of a face that was their metaphor of sleekness and all,
but I wanted no animal to confuse my human need.

I knew the disguised one was a usurper of the throne
whose true queen couldn't be hastened by wishes alone,
nor whose appearance could be foretold by diviners.

And coming third on the line mattered not to me in the order
of arrival. Who was ready to wait after two false alarms
would wait another month or year or more for his desire.

And then came the one dressed in simple elegance
without makeup and not striding as a Milan model;
she came with the splendour of dawn, fresh and rested.

She was bright like the stars that burned the night;
she carried herself in the pleasant gait of assurance
but could falter sometimes as every human did.

I was not expecting a goddess come to my world,
nor was I waiting for Mami Wata from her coral palace.
I knew my humanity was enough to hold us together.

She made me succumb to the rites
that would tie us as one, the destined pair.
She was mine to embrace forever.

Road Problems

When walking was the only means of covering distance
and the world knew I desperately wanted my bride,
they said a giant mahogany fell across the path she would take.
I had to pay with all I had for workers to hack it off the road.

But things did not work for decades I could not meet
demands that multiplied what was needed to have my way.
I wanted my bride every day more than any year before,
and I worked hard to seize the next chance I knew would come.

And then it came, though it took such a long time I had thought
all was over. The world knew that if I had been desperate years earlier
I would now be more than desperate to do its bidding to get my desire,
a rack I was struggling to free myself from every minute of my breath.

The news came that I could receive my bride in no time
but she would now come by car along roads that were tarred.
At first those bringing her complained of no fuel to drive the car.
Once I made sure the tank was filled to bring her from the world's end,

I was struck with another demand that was not unexpected:
the used car imported from Belgium broke down somewhere.
Nobody would like to pass the night with robbers and criminals
patrolling the road when lonely to rob and rape at random.

I did not have enough to send for the car to be repaired.
I was not sure whether the mechanic to be taken there
would not be one of the robbers that would destroy my desire.
I quickly learned the trade, not resting to achieve the task.

Today nobody knows how I got my bride after so many trials.
The world does not care about the debts I incurred along the way.
Only I knew what stood between me and my bride along the road
that would not easily give to me what I lived for to call mine.

In the Moonlight

I am not the only one out tonight.
Three women bare their breasts to me
and I can't help wondering what each expects
of me under the circumstances, a full moon.
Three different text messages in a quarter hour
with the same teasing theme confuse me.
Love is a labyrinth where we take refuge
from multiple assaults—whichever way
I take in the light will surely seek darkness.
I am not the only one out in the full moon;
the fruit ripened in a season of wild dreams.
Three possessed women bare their breasts
and I wonder what to do under the circumstances;
their texts with a taunting theme confuse me.

At Mambayya House, Kano

City esconsed in the savannah's bosom
tanned by an irreproachable sun
powdered dry by northerly winds
city smiling with kola nut-bleached teeth
marketplace of multiple tongues
crossroads of trade routes
where camel caravans deboard
and packed trucks converge
city of malams flourishing with reading
reverberating dawn to dusk with chants
city of arabesque and calligraphy
whose architecture tantalizes the eye
seven gated Old City citadel
Sabon Gari refuge of foreigners
city of tanneries of every hue
with leather Gucci would covet
draped with hand-woven cotton
Northern face of the nation
beach head of the Sahel
whose heat is tempered with cold
announcer of the harmattan's arrival
from its yearly sojourn to the Sahara
city of dust that boasts of a forest
city of rich farmers, herdsmen, and traders
refuge of fugitive Tuaregs and Buzus
oasis amidst drought-stricken lands
city where *bori* hides its songs
and durbar unleashes a pageant
city of emir and *talakawas*
city of Aminu Kano
lion policing the savannah
from menace of hyenas on the loose
in you polarities of lord and commoners

the fracas between faithful and kaffirs
igniting conflagrations in streets
in you the *talakawas* raise their voice
in NEPU[*] always reinventing itself
to break the outmoded mould.

---

[*] NEPU: Northern Elements Progressive Union, a radical party led by Aminu Kano.

After the Riots, in Jos

If they had butchered me as a Christian
they wouldn't have known

I had not entered a church to pray for decades
I had thrown away Moses and gone by the alias of Musa
I had seen real saints not canonized and many Catholic ones not saintly
I had convicted the Vatican for complicity in slave trade
and other crimes against humanity that still hurt deeply today
I had prayed for secular workers to take over the land's governance
to save the poor nation from prattling preachers and their businesses
I had trusted *igbe** worshipers to be friends and not born-again ones
I would rather be fed from the ancestral shrine than the church altar

if they had summarily executed me
they would have been more Catholic than the Pope
in silencing the chief Anti-Christ
whom he would have only excommunicated and left
alone to live outside the frontiers of the imperial faith
they would have committed haram
and martyred a humanist whose blood would cry high for vengeance

if they had slaughtered me as a kaffir for not being a fakir
they wouldn't know I affirm God is great to all believers
they would see no trace of wine turned blood on my tongue
no sugar from the cannibalized body of Jesus in my veins
no scent of incense on me from my associations
no verse of the Psalms on me as amulet against my enemies
no beads that contested with theirs for the power of prayers

---

* *igbe*: a traditional religious sect in Urhobo.

if they had quartered me
they wouldn't know their virtuous ones had given me my best love
I had chosen a bride from each cardinal point of the nation
I had stretched the measure of free will given me to escape
the ignorance that kept millions down when they should be up
and only the Merciful would show them justifiable anger
only the Great One would spite their monstrous souls
and only Allah knows the part of hell to place them eternally